Haywood County

Haywood County

A Brief History

Janet Threlkeld Webb

The History Press

Published by The History Press
Charleston, SC 29403
www.historypress.net

Cover image courtesy Janet Threlkeld Webb.

First published 2006

Manufactured in the United States

ISBN-13 978.1.59629.175.1

Library of Congress Cataloging-in-Publication Data

Webb, Janet Threlkeld.
Haywood County : a brief history / Janet Threlkeld Webb.
p. cm.
Includes bibliographical references.
ISBN-13: 978-1-59629-175-1 (alk. paper)
ISBN-10: 1-59629-175-3 (alk. paper)
1. Haywood County (N.C.)--History. 2. Haywood County (N.C.)--History--Anecdotes. 3. Haywood County (N.C.)--History, Local. 4. Haywood County (N.C.)--Biography. I. Title.
F262.H35W43 2006
975.6'94--dc22
2006023901

CONTENTS

Preface

In 1776, General Griffith Rutherford led soldiers through western North Carolina on a mission to subdue the Cherokee Indians. Many of them discovered a land where they would like to live and came back to these mountains, beginning in the 1790s. This book contains some of the stories of those who chose to live in western North Carolina.

As more folks came into the western part of the state, Haywood County was formed in 1808. The stories in this book are taken from the records of Haywood County, North Carolina. Then, as the population increased during the next sixty years, new counties were taken from the western and the southern part of Haywood County: Jackson, Macon and Swain Counties. In the 1810 census, Haywood County had 384 families within its boundaries. The original Haywood County extended from the Buncombe County line to the boundary of the Cherokee Indian Territory.

Commissioners were appointed for the purpose of selecting a place near the new county's center for public buildings in which to do the county's business. Other commissioners were selected to erect the courthouse, jail and stocks. The justices who lived in the county were to preside over the quarter sessions courts.

ACKNOWLEDGEMENTS

I want to thank Betsy Farlow, past president of the Haywood County Genealogical Society, for the encouragement to study the early deeds of Haywood County. It was this encouragement that led to the idea for the research of this book.

Thank you to my dear friend, Peggy Reeves Fugate, for reading this manuscript. She was a wonderful help and gave good suggestions as a proofreader.

To all the ancestors in Haywood County, we give our grateful acknowledgement for all the records that were recorded.

Thank you so very much, *Enterprise Mountaineer,* for giving permission to use pictures of old Waynesville, other old places in Haywood County and other pictures of interest.

Through all the research and writing of this book, the loving support of my husband, Francis, made it possible for me to continue the work. Without his support, I could not have taken on this project. I give him my heartfelt thanks.

Thank you to the editors at The History Press for your assistance in the preparation of this manuscript.

Haywood County: The Beginning

The Early History of Western North Carolina

The writings of William Bartram, Ora Blackmun and Michael Frome describe early western North Carolina. These writings inform us, who are removed by two hundred years of change, of the conditions faced by the pioneers who settled here in the beginning of this county. The nearest forestland that still resembles this wilderness is the Joyce Kilmer Forest.

American naturalist William Bartram described western North Carolina in his 1775 book *Travels of William Bartram*. He described the countryside as he crossed vales, ascended the high ridges of mountains, continued over gentler hills, narrow vales and lawns, fertile soils and verdant lofty forests. After ascending the Occonne Mountain, he rested. He wrote of the many types of trees and plants, the study of which was his main purpose for his trip. He related his encounters with the Cherokee people. Because the British encouraged the Cherokees to fight against the Americans in the early part of the Revolutionary War, Bartram decided to leave the area because of the possible dangers a white Patriot would have faced.

Additionally, Michael Frome relates William Bartram's travels in western North Carolina in the book *Stranger in High Places*. Frome provides maps and place names of Bartram's travels in North Carolina, including the descriptions of North Carolina's old growth forests, Indian-cleared meadows, fertile Cherokee farms, clean water in creeks and rivers and an abundance of wildlife.

For a long time, the Cherokee people held the land in Haywood County. The Cherokees had villages at the mouths of rivers, hunted in the lower parts of the mountains and rarely entered the high mountains. From the beginning of the Revolutionary War, the Cherokees sided with the British, raiding the frontier settlers who lived in the foothills on both sides of the mountains in North Carolina and Tennessee, killing, burning homes and destroying property.

The Patriots sent several military officers to put a stop to these raids, including General Griffith Rutherford, who led about 2,500 white soldiers and Catawba Indians in a march against the Cherokee towns. On September 1, 1776, the military left Fort Davidson and went by way of the Swannanoa Gap. They crossed the French Broad River and followed Hominy Creek past Enka. Next they went over the ridge (Pigeon Gap) to the Pigeon River and to its tributary, Richland Creek. (This took them past the area that would become Waynesville.) They continued to march on to the Tuckasegee River near Whittier and south over the Cowee Range to the Middle Villages of the Cherokees. When the job was done, they returned by the same route to Fort Davidson. General Rutherford had a burnt earth policy, destroying crops, orchards and homes. Many of the Cherokees who remained after the attacks died that winter from starvation and disease. Because they were so decimated from Rutherford's actions, the Cherokees saw no choice but to fight the British alongside the Patriots.

In the late 1780s after the war was over, the white soldiers remembered the good land in western North Carolina. They came and they settled. Because the white settlers were coming into the area in great numbers and making farms, clashes began between the new farming and traditional Cherokee hunting cultures. In the Holston Treaty of 1791, the Cherokee Indians gave up claims to the lands along the French Broad River near Asheville. Later, the Treaty of 1798 moved the lands of the Indian Territory westward.

After the pioneers arrived, the building of roads became very important. Cherokees had previously traveled in single file on paths created by the eastern bison. One of these, the Warpath, was a main thoroughfare in the Smokies. In Eastern Tennessee, the Warpath went through Hiwassee, Tellico and Chote to the mouth of the Tellico River, followed the river to Maryville, before heading down the Little River to Sevierville. After crossing the North Carolina state line, the Warpath continued north along the French Broad River. One branch of the Warpath went across Indian Gap down to Oconaluftee to the Tuckasegee River to Soco Gap and east into the area that was the watershed of Richland Creek.

These treaties moved the Indians ever westward. The lines drawn by the 1798 treaty stood at the western boundary of the present Haywood and Transylvania Counties. Then in 1838, the federal government tried to move all the Indians west of the Mississippi River. All the Cherokee Indians who left Georgia stayed in the west, but some Cherokees in North Carolina were able to remain. The descendants of these Indians make up the Eastern Tribe of the Cherokee.

ROBERT LOVE, FOUNDER OF WAYNESVILLE

Robert Love was a person of great ability from youth into old age. His copperplate handwriting gives evidence of his excellent education, and he rose high in the military ranks. An extremely successful businessman, Love was highly respected by his neighbors and provided a good education for his children. Unlike many of the other early pioneers, his sons went to college. He was active in local and state politics, and what he did two hundred years ago for the good of Haywood County continues to this very day.

Robert Love was born on May 11, 1760, to Samuel and Dorcas Bell Love, near the Tinkling Spring Meeting House in Augusta County, Virginia. His army career started in 1776 when he was about sixteen years old, ending in 1782 as a colonel. During the Revolutionary War, Robert served under Colonel Christie, one of the colonels in General Rutherford's 1776 campaign against the Cherokees. After the war, Colonel Love moved to Washington County in western North Carolina (an area that eventually became Tennessee).

On September 11, 1783, he married Mary Ann Dillard in what is now Erwin, Tennessee. He and Mary Ann had thirteen children: Thomas, Samuel, William, Dillard, John, James Robert, Sarah Jane, Ann, Winifred, Dorcas, Martha, Mary Anne and Rebecca. Before his tenth wedding anniversary, Love had moved his family to a home on the waters of Richland Creek, North Carolina, in 1792.

On Love's new estate, most of the land was wooded, but there was a nice Indian meadow in the bottomland. Until sawmills came into the area, homes were usually made of logs. Probably his home was two stories and had puncheon or wooden floors. An attic would have served as sleeping quarters for some of the family or servants, and a fireplace on the first floor would have been used for heating and cooking. Like most houses at the time, the windows had wooden shutters but no glass, which was difficult to ship safely. Log barns and outbuildings were for the keeping of farm equipment, storage of food for man and beast and for the servants' housing. Soon he would have a home that reflected his wealth and standing in the community.

Robert was a wealthy man. He had inherited a large fortune from his mother. Purchasing many acres of land throughout much of Haywood County, this land was productive and helped to increase his income. He was a land speculator, lawyer, justice of the peace and surveyor for part of the North Carolina state line. He was also a state senator and clerk of court in Haywood County for a number of years. Love gained a reputation as a soft-spoken gentleman who wore a split-tail coat, knee britches and silver buckles on his shoes in young adulthood, in contrast to the average man dressed in homemade cloth or leather.

One of the founding fathers of Haywood County and an active Presbyterian, Robert Love donated seventeen acres of his own land for the new town. Love was different than most of the other rich men of Haywood County, as he had a very large number of slaves. When he was fifty years old, he owned twenty-three slaves. As he accumulated new wealth, this increased to sixty slaves by the end of his life. In the last decade of his life, a fall from a horse caused him to be lame, and he had to use a walking stick until he died on July 17, 1845. Colonel Love was buried in Greenhill Cemetery in Waynesville. In the late 1900s the DAR donated a large stone monument on Love's grave, displaying his devotion to the county and the state.

Haywood County was named for John Haywood, the North Carolina state treasurer for many years. *Courtesy of the* Enterprise Mountaineer.

Right: Robert Love, the founder of Waynesville, North Carolina. *Courtesy of the* Enterprise Mountaineer.

Below: The unveiling of the marker placed on the courthouse grounds by the Daughters of the American Revolution after 1910. *Courtesy of the* Enterprise Mountaineer.

HOW HAYWOOD COUNTY CAME INTO BEING

An increasing number of people had taken up residence to the west of Asheville, and it became necessary to create a new county. The Buncombe County courthouse was far away for those living in the western North Carolina wilderness, and most men of the county had to attend the quarter courts to do important business. For those who lived in the very western part of the county, the several days' journey to Asheville involved travel on trails and paths up to sixty miles each way. This was very difficult during most of the year and almost impossible in the winter. Finally, on November 25, 1808, State Senator Thomas Love (Robert Love's brother) was influential in getting a bill passed in the General Assembly of North Carolina to create the new county of Haywood from the western lands of Buncombe County. The bill was ratified on December 23, 1808. Haywood was declared the newest county in North Carolina.

Thus, the boundaries were drawn for the new county, and all the active justices living in the new county were told by the General Assembly to participate in Haywood's Quarter Session Court. The county's eligible citizens had the privilege to vote in the federal elections. Taxes were levied for each poll and on the acreage of each landowner. Commissioners were appointed for the purpose of selecting a place near the new county's center. This was where the courthouse, jail and stocks would be built for county use. In 1809, Robert Love donated the land for Waynesville on a narrow sloping ridge of a hill about 1,320 feet southward from Robert's home. The deed for the town of Waynesville was finished on November 5, 1809. A surveyor plotted a main street, a cross street, a public square for the courthouse and jail as well as thirty lots of one half acre each. In January of 1810, the North Carolina General Assembly officially recognized the town.

The purpose of the courthouse was to conduct the business transactions of the county each quarter: Deeds were recorded for land and business deals. Provision was made for widows and orphans. Wills were registered and probated. Children were given into apprenticeship. Court orders were given for new roads to be built and older roads to be repaired. Disputes between people were settled. Any other civil needs were addressed. Officers for the business of the county were appointed or elected by the justices. These justices were esquires (men of property) who acted in the manner of a judge in civil matters. Occasionally, a jury was needed on one of the civil matters. Likewise, there was a Superior Court in which criminal cases were heard before a judge and a jury of men.

The justices who already lived in the territory that was now Haywood County were appointed to the county courts, including Thomas Love, John Fergus, John Dobson, Robert Phillips, Abraham Eaton, Hugh Davidson, Holliman Battle, John McFarland, Phillip T. Burford, William Deaver, Archibald McHenry and Benjamin Odle. Further instructions from the North Carolina General Assembly provided that the quarter session courts were to be held on the fourth Mondays of March, June, September and December in a place called Mount

Prospect. Thus the first Pleas and Quarter Session Court of the new county was held in March 1809. Because of his beautiful handwriting, Robert Love was elected Clerk of Court. He held this post for many years. Before June 1809, the county had received permission to hold court in the homes of John Howell, Robert Love and Holliman Battle (instead of Mount Prospect) until the county's courthouse could be built. The quarter session of the court that was to be held at the Battle home had to be moved to the John Welch home, as the record states, "out of necessity." However, after three years the courthouse was finally constructed and held its first court on December 21, 1812. A superior court was later established in the county.

The nearest town was Asheville and the only other villages were Indian settlements to the west of Waynesville. The people had lived in the area not much more than eighteen years when it was made a county. In the beginning, most travel ways were little more than paths, overgrown in summer and muddy in winter. Therefore, wagon road building was a large part of the business of the court.

Where the Justices Lived

When the pioneers—some of whom were men of education, money and high social standing—came to these mountains and valleys, they used their wealth to establish homes in the style of the times. Some farms belonging to one man could be located in many different valleys across the county. They would have the necessary buildings to maintain the farm. This was not a settlement where a different number of people would own small lots for a business or a house as in town.

The justices of the Haywood County court were men of great means and lived throughout the county. This section will show the great distances that some of the men had to travel to do the work of the court. The deeds that were recorded in the court indicate where the justices may have lived or where they farmed or conducted business.

Thomas Love lived on the land adjacent to Richland Creek near his older brother, Robert. This waterway drains the hills and valleys of this southern part of Haywood County. Two other court justices, Holliman Battle and David Powell, lived on Richland Creek near the Love brothers. Later, Battle had a home in Waynesville.

South of Waynesville, Phillip T. Burford had a home on Raccoon Creek. Another justice, Benjamin Odle (or Odell), had a home on Scotts Creek across Balsam and a home in Waynesville.

To the west, John Fergus had places on Scotts Creek and Oconaluftee in Cherokee. John Mingus lived in Cherokee. A gristmill called the Mingus Mill was near his home. Mingus Mill was on the western side of the villages of the Cherokee Indians that were on the Oconaluftee River.

Returning to central Haywood County, Robert Phillips lived on the Big Pigeon River. This area was called the Warpath Ford of Pigeon until about 1900

The old Bon Air Hotel on Main Street, Waynesville, 1920s. *Courtesy of the* Enterprise Mountaineer.

The complex of the Gordon Hotel, 1930. *Courtesy of Janet Webb.*

when it became Canton. There were very few homes there in the early years. The area at the ford had too much swampy land. This ford was near where the paper mill plant was later built.

John McFarland had a home in a wild and beautiful area called the east fork of Pigeon River, later called Cruso. On the west fork of the Pigeon River lived William Deaver, near what was known as Deaver's Gap. Deaver's Gap may be the Pigeon Gap.

Turning to the north, Hugh Davidson settled on Jonathan Creek and had land on Mount Sterling. Between Mount Sterling and Jonathan Valley across the Cataloochee Divide are the valleys of Little Cataloochee and Cataloochee. These two valleys eventually became a part of the National Park System. Jonathan Creek is a broad, well-watered valley, perfect for farming. This was one of the earliest parts of the county to be settled. Across Utah Mountain to the east was Crabtree Valley. The main creek was Crabtree Creek where Archibald McHenry lived. All these creeks flow into waterways that finally drain into the Mississippi River to the west. No water flows into Haywood County.

These additional men served the court system. Abraham Eaton was added to the list of justices on March 29, 1809. At this same time Robert Phillips resigned as a justice. Thomas McClure took the oath of justice of peace on June 1811. David Russell's name was added to the list of the justice of peace for a short time.

Therefore, these men traveled miles to come to Waynesville on court days. Some of the earliest items of business of the court were to set up road crews.

After Main Street was paved, circa 1905. The bank on the right side of the picture was the First Union National Bank. *Courtesy of the* Enterprise Mountaineer.

The working hands of these crews were possibly the employees or slaves of the men who lived on the routes of the roads to be made or improved. The court would stress "the easiest and best way" from a given place to where the road was to be completed. The first choice of a place for a road was the Indian path designed by the eastern bison, which only rarely crossed the mountain gaps. The gap of a mountain caused a crooked road, as the road had to follow the shape of the side of the mountain. These roads were built by hand with shovels and picks. There were two types of roads, a standard road and the broader wagon road. Thus, any wagon road built across the gap had to be wide enough for the wagon to get through the curve without falling down the mountain or off an embankment.

Traveling on and helping to build these early roads, most men in the county had to do business in the court. This was a very important part of their lives. As the court met only every four months, all the men eligible to attend court sessions would for both business and social reasons.

THE PEOPLE OF HAYWOOD COUNTY

Who were the people of Haywood County and what did they accomplish? First, we know they built homes and worked to provide a living for their families. When people first came to western North Carolina, the only educational possibilities for children were home schooling by the parents or, in the case of the well-to-do, a tutor or boarding school outside of the local area. Although there were public and private schools in more populated areas of North Carolina, it was several years before the state system was widely established. Some of the first schools were held in the local church and the teacher was the minister. One of the main purposes of learning to read was to be able to read the Bible. It was also important to be able to do math. The state law required that "reading and ciphering was to be taught to the youngsters who were bondservants or in apprenticeship." One county resident, William H. Thomas, was educated at home and later made his own living. His father died before he was born, but his mother taught him at home, so that when he was in his mid-teens he was doing business in a store.

As such people grew older, the records of their lives were written down and stored in the courthouse. These documents—such as those determining the exact bounds of property lines or wills for passing on property—were necessary to the business of everyday life and made Haywood County's early existence orderly and lawful. Even for those who could not write, knowing how to tell a lawyer what was to be in the document was of greatest importance.

These documents contain the stories about a few of the people who lived in Haywood County. These people are the ancestors of many of the people who are living in this part of the state today. One only has to look at the local telephone book to see the family names that are still here. These names and

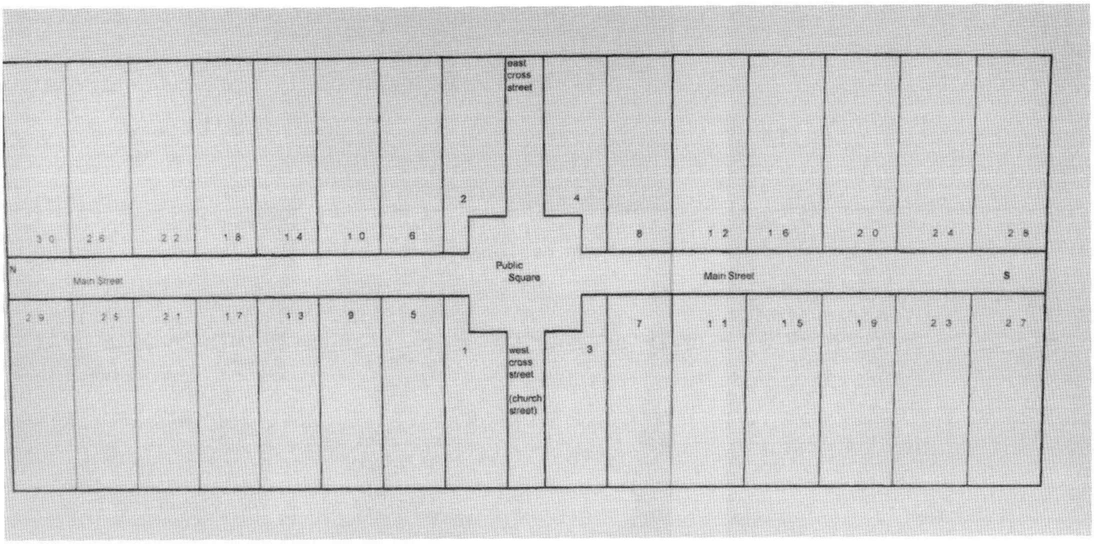

The first plot map of Waynesville, 1830. *Courtesy of the Haywood County Register of Deeds.*

the little that is revealed about them in each will may be the only information that is known about a particular family. Others' activities were archived in public records. These were the pioneers who worked hard to survive and to make a place for their children. In the stories of life and death found in a will, it is possible to have a greater understanding of our ancestors as they helped to develop a new county. Some of this information tells of the country of the first settlers' origin and if they were able to read or write.

In addition to the will, the list of inventories revealed the financial standing of a family. The settlement of an estate, even when there was not a will, provided a year in which the person probably died. A close friend, sometimes along with the wife of the deceased, became administrators of the will and inventories. In some of the inventories, the names of those who bought the items of the personal estate were listed. These names may have included the wife and children. One example of this was John Hughes: his wife and a friend were the administrators of his estate and his children bought some items.

The first two families named in Haywood County's records were Jones and Hollingsworth. Records for the Hollingsworth family were not as clear, but Robert Jones wrote a will on August 28, 1808. Robert was a farmer. There was no record of a deed, and in his will he left only personal property. His friend, William Fraser and son, G. Washington Jones, witnessed his will, while his wife, Mary Ann Jones, and his son Abyram were his executors. His five sons were John, Abyram, George Washington, Marsell and Reason (deceased) and his four daughters, Betsy, Bathsheba, Nancy and Polly. This will was probated in the court's June 1809 session. When examining these facts of the family's lives and deaths, one wonders where this Jones family lived, how long they had lived in Haywood before Robert died and how long the children stayed in Haywood County following his death. In the 1810 census, Mary was over forty-five years of age. One son was about grown and three boys were small children. Of the girls in this census, the oldest may be nearly grown. This was the last mention of this family and it is likely that the Joneses moved on after the head of the household had died.

Other early Haywood County documents reveal the large families that were common in the early 1800s. John Johnson, who wrote his will January 17, 1824, was married to a woman named Prissiller and died in 1825. According to the 1820 census, he was over forty-five years of age. He had eight children, two of whom were named Daniel and Westly. There were seven or eight dependents (either children or grandchildren) in his home in 1820, at least two males and five females.

Many citizens who could not read signed their names with a mark. George Barns signed his name with an X. According to his will, Drusilla and he had five children: Mary, William, Morning, Nelly (who married a man with the last name Burrel) and George, as well as at least two grandsons, Andrew and Niniany, from his daughter Mary. After George became sick, a lawyer helped him write his will on February 10, 1825, before he died in 1826. Robert Ferguson also used a mark (O) to sign his name on his will, dated February 18, 1820. His wife, Janney, and he had three sons—William, Thomas and Samuel—and two daughters. Robert died eight years after he made his will.

A gathering to encourage the paving of Main Street, Waynesville. This 1900 photo depicts the view across from the courthouse. *Courtesy of the* Enterprise Mountaineer.

North Main Street, 1892. *Courtesy of the* Enterprise Mountaineer.

Mrs. Lula Felmet's boardinghouse on Main Street across from the rock bank building, 1908. *Courtesy of the* Enterprise Mountaineer.

The first building of the Grace Episcopal Church built in 1880. *Courtesy of the* Enterprise Mountaineer.

The first Waynesville High School near the First Methodist Church, February 1869. *Courtesy of the* Enterprise Mountaineer.

Another family head, Samuel Hollingsworth, was ill when he wrote his will on January 3, 1810, although he had been able to do business on June 5, 1809, by witnessing a deed for a friend. The will was probated in the March Session of 1810. He only mentions his wife, Elisabeth, his youngest son, Enoch, and two daughters, Margaret and Ruth. The other children must have had their own homes, as they are not in the 1810 census. In the census of 1810, Enoch is listed as the head of the household of three people, two of whom were over forty-five years of age. Samuel left real estate to his heirs. It does not appear that this family registered the deed to their land.

Next are a few more families—Cabe, Patterson, Rogers and Parham—who were listed in wills. John Cabe wrote a will on April 24, 1810 and it was probated in the same year. He named both children and grandchildren and was probably a widower. His oldest daughter, Mary and her husband, Thomas Stiles had children, Catherine and John. John Cabe's son, John, had a son named John. Also, his other sons, James and Zechariah each had sons named John. Joseph was the son of Stephen Cabe who was deceased. He had another grandson, Amos Cabe. Then there was a man named Samuel Patterson. He died in 1814.

How many of the families whose last names are in these wills know the stories of their ancestors? Which ancestors passed down their histories? In the written records, these brief biographical notes are the only bits of data known about these first Haywood County folks.

Waynesville and Richland Creek

Little Waynesville

When Haywood County was created on November 19, 1808, Robert Love had promised to deed a plot of land for the courthouse and public buildings in the county seat. Donating a little more than seventeen acres for this purpose, he stated that this was "for the good will and esteem that he hath and bearth to the citizens of the said county of Haywood." The deed was completed on November 5, 1809, and registered in the December session of court in 1811. The North Carolina General Assembly recognized Waynesville as the first town in Haywood County in 1810.

When Love had the property surveyed, it contained Main Street, Cross Street, thirty half-acre lots and a public square of about an acre. Love instructed the surveyor to build a road 1,320 feet southwest of his home. This would have been a difficult job for the surveyor, as he would have been working in an old growth timber situation on a narrow ridge and sloping land. All the large timber and bushes had to be cleared from Main Street, Cross Street and the public square. With axes to remove the trees, workers of that day only had hand tools, horses, oxen, mules and muscles with which to remove the stumps.

When the survey was finished, the width of Main Street was about 58 feet wide and the length was about 1,039 feet long with woodlands on either end. Main Street went up the crest of the ridge towards the south. Halfway up the street, Cross Street was 49 feet wide and 586 feet long. The width and length of the streets in the beginning had to fit into the seventeen acres of Robert Love's deed. The widths of these two streets have not changed in two hundred years. The length of these short streets began to expand as the court ordered road building that was developed over the years.

The LaFaine Hotel, 1925. *Courtesy of Janet Webb.*

An early view of North Main Street and Walnut Street, Waynesville. The Presbyterian church is on the left and the Gordon Hotel is on the right, 1890. *Courtesy of the* Enterprise Mountaineer.

A steam engine at the depot in Waynesville, shortly after 1900. *Courtesy of the* Enterprise Mountaineer.

Before this street was built, the whole area must have been wooded in old growth timber, and this aspect of the wilderness remained as it was for nearly one hundred years until Main Street was paved with brick. The original red clay surface lies eighteen inches below the pavement. Pictures of Main Street dated before 1904 display a dirt road lined with large maple trees.

Taking a panoramic view of the mountains around Waynesville for 360 degrees, the following sights are visible: Looking northwest across the valley and small knolls is the long ridge of Eagles Nest Mountain, first known as Mount Junaluska. From the north down Main Street, Chambers Mountain takes center stage. Because of the upward slope of Main Street to the south, it is impossible to see the Balsam Range and Lickstone Ridge dominates the southeastern view. Lickstone Ridge divides the Waynesville valley from the valley of the west fork of Pigeon River. At the north end of Lickstone Ridge, you can see a gap near Ratcliff Mountain visible from Waynesville, named Pigeon Gap. (There is not a Deaver's Gap on the map, and it may be that Deaver's Gap is another name for Pigeon Gap.) This valley on the waters of Richland Creek has many little hills. The highest hill in the center of this valley was where Robert Love had a home and wrote the deed for the town of Waynesville.

Although the Waynesville post office was established on March 14, 1831 (with Ruben Deaver as the first postmaster), Waynesville remained a small town for a long time. After the Civil War there were only about fifteen families in the town and about seventy-five people, two stores and the Battle House Hotel. At this point, on the southern end of Main Street was the home of Judge Gudger. On the northwestern end of Main Street was the home of William Ray, where eventually Doctor R.L Allen lived.

THE ENLARGING OF WAYNESVILLE

After sixty years of existence, Waynesville began to grow. In 1871 the town was incorporated with a population of a little fewer than two hundred people. In 1878 the White Sulfur Springs Hotel was opened and the advertisement of "the land of the sky" came into being. In 1880 a new courthouse was built, this time of brick. It was located on the land where the present courthouse stands. When the railroad was completed in 1882, the North Carolina Teachers Assembly met at the White Sulfur Springs Hotel. Beginning in 1890 and continuing for a number of years many hotels were built in the area. Attracting visitors with a love of the mountainous setting, this was the beginning of Waynesville as a tourist haven.

In 1885 the following buildings were added to Waynesville: the *Waynesville Courier*, some drugstores, a plumbing business and additional churches. In 1887 Alden Howell built a bank, and a charter for the First National Bank was granted on December 26, 1902, to be built on Main Street. Some of the men involved in this included Clyde H. Ray, Charles E. Ray, S.C. Satterthwait, Dr. J. Howell Way and Samuel C. Welch. By 1906, the Commercial Bank opened with R.E. Osborn as the president.

As a result of economic growth, new institutions for improving the quality of life were introduced. In the 1890s, a library association was organized; graded schools started with 240 students and electric lights were installed. As Waynesville continued to grow, hotels and boarding houses were built. Some of them were the Gordon Hotel, the Bon Air and Mrs. Mark Felmet's boarding house. Then, the Battle House Hotel became the Waynesville Inn and the National Hotel, built by 1896, became the Dunham Hotel. An annex was added to the White Sulfur Springs Hotel to accommodate the growing crowds. On the crest of Mount Junaluska the Eagles Nest Hotel was built, and the Waynesville side of Mount Junaluska began to be referred to as Eagles Nest Mountain, while the Dellwood side was Mauney Cove. By 1903 public water was installed, and Main Street was finally paved in 1904. A brick post office was built on the corner of Main Street and Church Street, and Frank W. Miller was its first postmaster in 1917.

Opposite bottom: The Sulphur Spring for which the hotel was named. This is the only remaining structure after the hotel burned. This picture was taken in 1990. *Courtesy of the* Enterprise Mountaineer.

Above: The White Sulphur Springs Hotel, which was first built as the home of James Robert Love (son of Robert Love), was burned in 1877 and rebuilt as a hotel. This annex was added with the rise of the hotel's popularity. *Courtesy of the* Enterprise Mountaineer.

Wealthy guests made a five-mile drive up Mount Junaluska after they departed from the train in Waynesville before reaching the Eagles Nest Hotel, a lavish summer hotel owned by Samuel C. Satterthwaite, 1899. *Courtesy of Janet Webb.*

Carriages of pleasure waiting for guests to arrive from New York and Jacksonville, Florida, 1900. *Courtesy of the* Enterprise Mountaineer.

HERE THE BUILDINGS WERE

Examining old fire insurance maps, one can see the original layout of downtown Waynesville. One woman told me that as she read about these old structures, she remembered when she was a young girl living in Waynesville. It brought back many happy memories. If you, reader, did not see these yesteryear streets, perhaps you can use your imagination to recognize the changes that have taken place.

Down Church Street from the southwest corner of Main, there were only three private homes in 1896, but these three homes and all other buildings were gone from this section by 1908 until the post office was built in 1917. A livery and transfer, a large building on the corner of Church and Haywood facing Montgomery Street, joined the post office on the map as the only two buildings on Church Street in 1924. In 1931, the two new structures were the Masonic Temple and another building attached to the large building on the corner. The town hall, temple building, parking lots and the Waynesville Towers apartments make up this section in 2006.

On the other side of Church Street from the northwest corner of Main Street, only one home stood on the maps in 1896, 1908 and 1913. By 1924, a drugstore had appeared on the corner on Main and Church Streets, along with several small businesses and a garage for carriages and cars on the corner of Montgomery Street. At the intersection of Main and Church Streets, the building now houses a kitchen shop in 2006. There are several other small businesses of interest with a restaurant called the Lomo Grill on the corner of Church and Montgomery Streets.

North Main Street before 1920. *Courtesy of the* Enterprise Mountaineer.

On the west side of South Main Street from Church Street to Academy Street, the Battle House Hotel stood in the second lot in 1896. Down the street, there were several small business buildings next to a private home. The last two buildings on the street were the National Hotel and the Baptist church. In 1908 and 1913, the Hotel Waynesville had sprung up on the end of the block, followed by a plumbing business, another business and two homes. The National Hotel still stood with the Baptist church on the corner. In 1924 and 1931 on this same large piece of property were the following buildings: the post office, Hotel Waynesville, a garage for carriages and cars, a house, the Dunham Hotel and the First Baptist Church, with three homes behind the church on Academy Street. In 2006, the corner building has become the Town Hall, with businesses dotting the street. All the way to the corner of South Main and Academy Street is the First Baptist Church complex.

On east side of South Main Street from East Street to Pigeon Street, there were not many buildings in 1896 on this lot. The next five buildings were a general store with a house nearby, another home, and a second general store, followed by a house. There was a vacant building, two liveries and a stable yard on the corner of Pigeon Street. On the next block beyond Pigeon Street remains the Dr. Joseph Howell Way home and office. In 1908 from the corner of East Street, there were the following buildings: a general store, a livery, a barber, a tailor, a restaurant, a plumber, another general store, a private home and a skating rink on the corner of South Main Street and Pigeon Street. However, after a murder was committed there, the skating rink closed. In 1913 the fire station was on the street edge. There were two general stores and the P.L. Turbyfill Livery on the corner of this lot. In 1924 and 1931, the corner of South Main Street and East Street contained a number of buildings, some of which were a store, a garage and city hall. The next group of buildings contained the fire station. There was a garage in the attached large building. Finally, on the corner of Main Street and Pigeon Street was an Esso Gas Station. Today, 2006, the police station, fire station, a large building next to a parking lot and a large gas station and market make up this block. In another year or so, the fire station will no longer be in this location. Because more space is needed for the fire station it will soon be located in another part of town, on North Main Street.

This part of Main Street is on the West Side of North Main Street from Church Street to Depot Street. In 1896, there were a few buildings on the first lot, a home on the second lot and nothing on lot three. The lot before a driveway contained the Roger house and the Red Wing Gift Shop general store. In the middle of the next lot in a series of buildings was a hardware store. The following

Opposite top: The Moody House on Main Street, Waynesville, early 1900s. *Courtesy of the* Enterprise Mountaineer.

Opposite bottom: The corner where the post office was built in Waynesville. The house on the far left is the Battle House and Hotel. December 1, 1916. *Courtesy of the* Enterprise Mountaineer.

lot contained a home and well at the street edge. There was a bank in the little rock building, which is still in use on Main Street. Next to the last lot contained a private home, and the corner lot had only a vacant building on it. In 1908, the Kenmore Hotel, which had previously been the home of Dr. Horace Wells, was next to the rock bank; the county jail was back of the hotel. The little brick doctor's office was next to a private home. In the last lot were an empty building and the bank on the corner of Depot Street. By 1913, the hardware store had become a furniture store, the rock bank was a library and the vacant house next to the bank was a boardinghouse. Below the bank on Depot Street were three office buildings. In 1924 the first block was filled with five buildings. A furniture store was transformed into a movie theater, the Kenmore Hotel had added an annex and the boardinghouse next to the bank on the corner had been replaced by a very small office. The following year, the furniture store and movie theater building became the Massie building. Even more changes affected this section by 1931. The second lot had two new businesses, lot number three had a new large store and a drugstore and Miller Street had been built between the Roger house and the Red Wing Gift Shop general store. The Kenmore Hotel building was empty. The very small office next to the bank became a larger building.

Dr. Joseph Howell Way's home and office in about 1900. *Courtesy of the* Enterprise Mountaineer.

The old Kenmore Hotel shortly before it closed in 1929. *Courtesy of the* Enterprise Mountaineer.

The Kenmore Hotel was first the home of Dr. Horace Wells on Main Street. 1908. Dr. Wells recorded the 1880 organizational meeting of the Haywood County Board of Health. *Courtesy of the* Enterprise Mountaineer.

When this photo was taken shortly after 1903, East Street was blocked off by businesses. The P.L. Turbyfill Livery Stable was one of the businesses in the picture. Today this is where the police station is located. *Courtesy of the* Enterprise Mountaineer.

In this same section of town in 2006, there are many businesses including art galleries, furniture stores, clothing stores, a bank, a restaurant and a lawyer's office on the corner of Depot Street. Miller Street starts about halfway down this side of the street. The old building on Miller Street that housed the Red Wing Gift Shop is now gone, the old rock building is a Christmas gift store and the little brick doctor's office is the L.N. Davis Insurance office. Where the bank on the corner once stood is now a lawyer's office.

In 1896 the east side of North Main Street, beginning at East Street and ending in front of the county courthouse, boasted a vacant store, a private home and the Willis House (with a well in the side yard). A photo business, operated by G.D. Sherrill, resided on this street, as well as millinery in a wooden building by itself. General stores, a bookstore, the Bank of Waynesville and another general store stood next to two homes, one of which was Lula Felmet's boardinghouse. After this there were four separate buildings facing Depot Street. The first building was the Chautagua Drug Store owned by McIntosh and Ford, which may have been the old Allen Drug Store, possibly one of the oldest buildings on Main Street. The next two businesses were a general store and a liquor store. According to the 1908 map, a bakery and a general store were where the Whitman's Bakery and Sandwich Shop are today. The second home was the Willis homeplace, along with a doctor's office and a photo shop. The millinery, a furniture store and a bank were the buildings located across from the old Red Wing Gift Shop and the

Massie Store. There were two private homes across the street from the rock bank. A restaurant faced the brick doctor's office and there was a small office building sitting by itself in the middle of the next block. In the next eight buildings, some of the businesses were a stationery store, photo shop, two drugstores and a liquor store. By 1913, the photo shop became a movie theater. A barber and pool hall sporting club and several other businesses had replaced the restaurant. The little office was made into two larger offices. A jewelry store had replaced the liquor store. In the changes of 1924, the building on the corner of East Street was enlarged. The big bank building had replaced the millinery shop, and a fifth store had been added to this group of buildings. The second house across from the Kenmore Hotel was replaced by a group of buildings, the first of which was a pool hall, followed by a movie theater. In the last group of buildings a pool hall had replaced the photo shop. In 1934 a large store building filled in the gap between the last two blocks of buildings. In 2006, the whole of the street from East Street to the little one-way street next to the newspaper offices contains a solid row of businesses. The only breaks in this solid row are two alleys, which are still in use.

The west side of North Main Street from Depot Street to Walnut Street contained the brick courthouse and Court Place Drive beside a private home in 1896. The next building, the Reeves Hotel, had a detached kitchen. Finally, a private home and the Presbyterian church made up this section. From at least 1908 to 1913, this section was the courthouse, an expanded Court Place Drive that was seventeen feet wide (which went beyond the private home), a very small office near the Windsor Hotel and a larger private home next to the church. By 1924 the Windsor Hotel became a store, and the street grew more residential as there were five homes on Walnut Street between the Presbyterian church and Branner Street. In 1931, the store had become the Hotel LaFaine with a filling station next door. The Tate Home (Towne House) and the Presbyterian church completed this block. Presently, the courthouse complex containing the new justice center and the Presbyterian church occupies the entire block.

Further down on the east side of North Main Street, beginning at the one-way street between the newspaper office and a store facing Depot Street, private homes and small offices made up this section in 1896. In 1908, the first building across from the courthouse was a private home. Next was a hardware business along with a few offices. The Bon Air boardinghouse was next. A private home and the Gordon Hotel completed this section. In 1913, the only building that was missing was the newspaper office and there was no little street, which were built in 1931. This area remains largely unchanged in 2006. The *Enterprise Mountaineer* newspaper complex, a drive-through alley, the former Coffee Hardware Store and offices run the length of the street, with a funeral home, a lighting business and a furniture store are all set back from the street with the parking lots in front of the businesses.

In 1908, on the south corner of Church Street and Haywood Street was a printing business. Depot Street crossed Richland Creek on an iron bridge. The street in front of the train station next to the side tract was called Railroad Street. On the corner of Depot Street and Haywood Street was a livery. The

Waynesville High School on Haywood Street faced Academy Street and was next to the Methodist church. The Grace Episcopal Church was on Haywood Street. On the corner lot next to it facing Church Street was a large private home. In 1924, the Waynesville Township High School was located where the

The Battle Hotel was on the lot next to the post office. This hotel later became the Waynesville Hotel. This sketch was made in 1879. *Courtesy of the* Enterprise Mountaineer.

middle school is today. The old high school building on Haywood Street is gone; Central Elementary School was built in its place. Today it is the building in which the Landmark Apartments were located.

THE ORIGINAL MAIN STREET OF WAYNESVILLE

After Robert Love founded and began construction on the town of Waynesville, John Welch bought thirteen lots in 1811, although he did not develop most of them. The newly cleared landscape of Waynesville did not change very much in the next few years. However, Welch along with Jesse Anderson did establish "a house of public entertainment" on August 16, 1810 (on what is now South Main Street beyond the present Police Station), shortly after buying these lots. Local residents could have a drink, eat a meal, learn the news and get a night's sleep in a building that may have contained only two rooms. One of the twelve by sixteen foot rooms would serve as the main room and the other, a place for sleeping. Some may have chosen to roll up in a blanket or bear skin and spend the night on the floor in front of the fireplace in the main room. Anderson and Welch quit their business dealings in 1812. Court records revealed that many people sued Anderson for debts he owed. Also, John Welch had a trading company that carried supplies to the territory of Missouri. Welch Street, one block off of Main Street, now divides the length of some of his original lots.

In the original Waynesville, the public square had the first log jail, exercise yard and stocks near the present police station, with the addition of the log

The post office shortly after it was built, 1917. *Courtesy of the* Enterprise Mountaineer.

courthouse in 1812. Benjamin Chambers built a house and a store on the corner lot next to the jail. The jail and Chambers's store each crossed the property line, but the town and Chambers made a mutual agreement concerning the disputed land under each building. Also, paths were used across lots as shortcuts instead of going to Cross Street. About ninety years later, Cross Street became two streets, Church Street and East Street.

A Mr. Jones lived next door to Love's storehouse (which Jesse Anderson built) on the northeast side of Main Street. Love later moved into a house nearby, close to a present-day Christian bookstore. Fences, wells and an open-air market were also part of the original Waynesville Main Street. On the west side of Main Street, William Welch built a house and planted an orchard. This location is now the lower parking lot of the First Baptist Church. A house and leather shop were next on the street. Next to this was the rock house that Samuel Fitzgerald built and lived in by himself. A typical house of the day, it was about sixteen by twenty feet. Such rock houses were cool in the summer, but chilly in the winter, so across the room from the bed was a good fireplace. In front of the fireplace was a table where he ate and worked, and stored on the mantel were tin plates, spoons and cups. One small window was set in the foot-thick wall. A good well was dug a few feet from his front door.

The following lot on the western side of the public square is where Holliman Battle built his home in Waynesville. Holliman Battle was the son of John and Ann Holliman Battle. He was born on November 8, 1772, in eastern North Carolina. His father died when he was five years old. His mother remarried to John Fergus when he was ten years old. Holliman married Elizabeth, and their children were James Madison Battle, William Wayne Battle and Henry Van

The Dunham House was a popular summer hotel in the 1920s. *Courtesy of Janet Webb.*

Battle. Holliman's son Henry died when he was two years old. Holliman was postmaster in 1816 and 1820. It was in 1840 that he moved to Georgia. The Battle House was enlarged to become a hotel so that it would be welcoming guests by the time the trains began to arrive in Waynesville.

Activity on Main Street increased when court was in session. Riders arrived from all parts of the county and they tied their horses at the hitching rails. Everyone was interested in the proceedings: registering of deeds for land and business agreements, appointing powers of attorney, providing for a widow and her children from her deceased husband's estate, directions for a new wagon road and breakings of the law. For those who could not get into the courtroom, the doorway served as a listening post. To listen to the oratory of lawyers was a source of entertainment.

A traveler who stopped in Waynesville prior to 1880 called it "a dirty little rude village." The street was red clay and dust settled on everything nearby. Sometimes the rain would continue for days! A man could sink to his ankle in the red mud. A sucking sound was heard for each foot lift when one was walking on wet red clay. The hooves of horses and oxen as well as the narrow wagon wheels had churned the street into mire. Another sound was heard if a fall occurred instead of a step. Then, upon the gentleman's return home, the work of removing the red mud from boot and pant leg was a major operation.

Little by little the town began to grow. More homes and businesses were built on Main Street. This type of slow progress continued for about seventy years until the railway was built from Asheville to Waynesville. About this time Main Street became longer and shortly thereafter a new brick courthouse was built in a new location further North on Main Street, the present location of the courthouse and justice center. It was the train that encouraged the building of fine hotels. The families of the businessmen of the lowlands of North Carolina and South Carolina came for the summer because of the healthy climate. In the very early 1900s the summer folks would swell the population from a few thousand to five or six times as many people. This gave additional income to the local people. This was and still is a beautiful land.

The Lots of Main Street

There were many articles that have been written about the different homes and businesses on Main Street. It was a real challenge to search the deeds and make a deed chain from the beginning of Waynesville into modern times. The following article is the result of part of this deed search.

The standard size of the half-acre lots were 82½ feet wide and 264 feet long, with the exception of the four corner lots which had a corner of 33 feet by 66 feet to be used for part of the public square. The lot numbers were alternating from each side of the street and each side of the public square as is shown in the town map.

Lot number one was located on the northwest corner of the square. The first owner of this lot was state senator and Haywood County founding father Thomas Love.

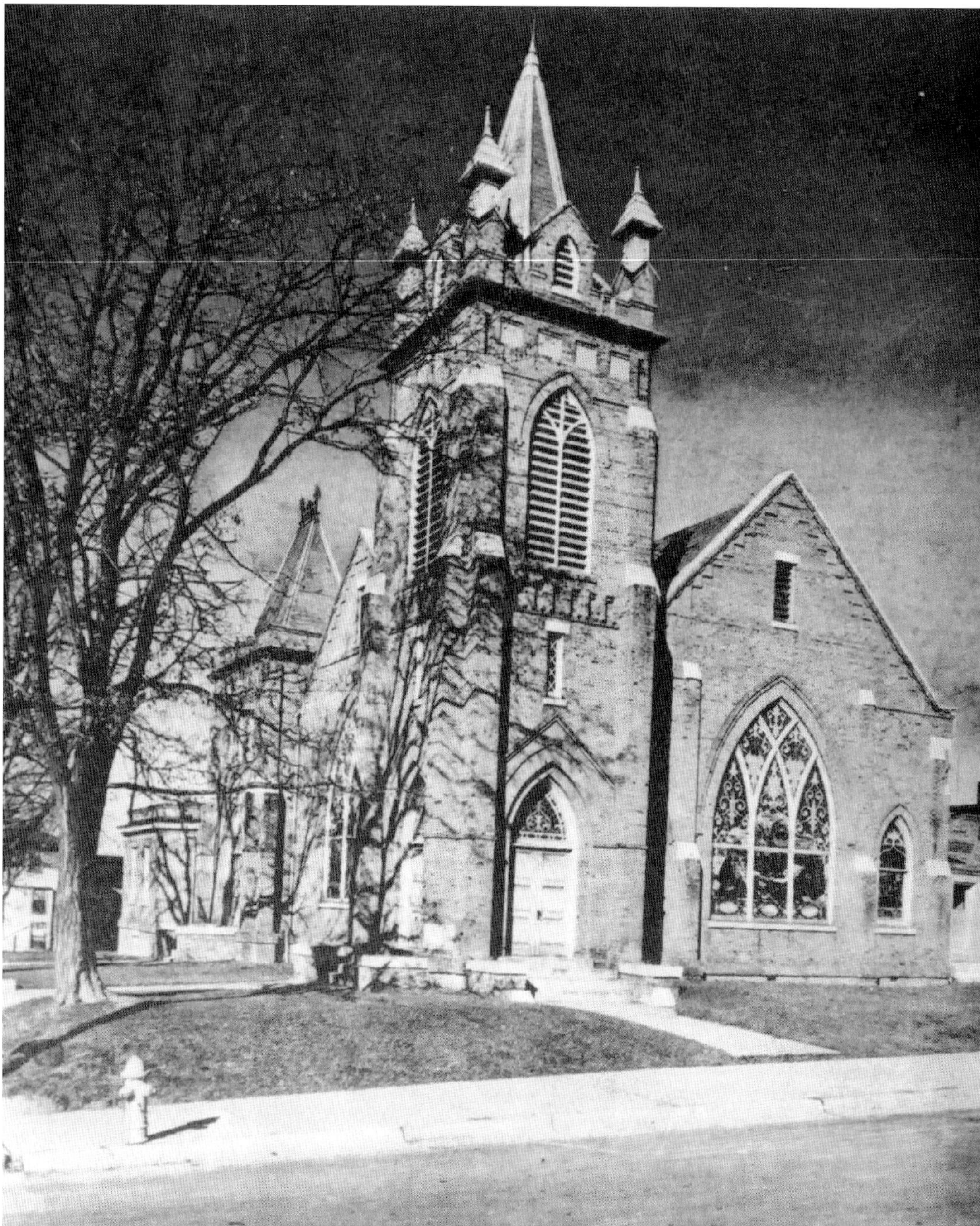

The First Baptist Church in the 1940s. *Courtesy of Janet Webb.*

Thomas was born in Virginia and served under General George Washington in the American Revolutionary War. Settling in the part of Buncombe County that became Haywood County, he eventually made one of his homes on this lot in Waynesville. He lived in Haywood County for about thirty years before moving to Tennessee where he died in 1830. By 1834 this lot was known as Fostel's lot. Willard Howell owned it or a part of it in 1893. Today, the first business on the corner is the kitchen shop; there are other businesses that fill out the rest of the lot.

Lot number two was located on the northeast corner of the square. This was one of the lots that John Welch bought in 1811. By 1825, Josiah A. Bird owned the lot, but the sheriff, James McKee, sold it because Bird was in debt to Robert Love and William Welch. William Welch was married to Mary Ann Love, the daughter of Robert Love. In 1831 William and Hugh Johnson became owners. Then it belonged to Robert Love and William Welch in 1842. Currently, this is where the Gateway store and Whitman's Bakery and Sandwich Shop are located.

Lot number three was located on the southwest corner of the square and was originally owned by James R. Love, the son of Robert Love. Elias Jarrett bought it in 1834, selling it to Francis McGee in 1837. Mr. E.S. Howell had it for a while. Then Samuel Fitzgerald bought it in 1843. In 1873 a front portion of the lot was sold. The building that is located next to the Town Hall is where the Holliman Battle house was originally located. The other part of the public square next to what is now Church Street was where the Waynesville post office was located before it became the town hall. This part of Cross Street was renamed Church Street.

Benjamin Chambers owned a store on the southeast corner lot next to the town square in 1830. By 1881 it was owned by John K. Boone. The Martin Electric Company was on this corner lot. Also, the Baptist Church bought a portion of it for a parking lot.

This is the corner of the square on which the jail was first built. This is where the police station and fire department are located today. In the late 1800s, the courthouse was moved from its location on the square to its present location. That part of the square where the courthouse had first been built was sold as lots, including the entrance to East Cross Street. In 1900 the entrance to East Cross Street was relocated a little to the north of the original street and renamed East Street. This reopening of East Street eliminated several of these temporary lots.

Further down Main Street, lot number nine on the northwest side of the street was one of the Welch lots in 1811. Over the years, other owners of at least a part of this lot were Aaron Britton, Ruben Deaver, Harvey Kilby, James T. Kilby, S.C. Satterthwait, James Cox, H.B. Atkins, H.A. Ford, before passing into the Massie family in 1925. The Massie family owned a furniture business, which included providing caskets for the deceased although this part of the business ceased when the funeral homes began to provide this service. The Massie furniture store is still located at 18 Main Street and is still in the Massie family.

The last portion of the last lot number twenty-nine on the northwest side of the street is the parking lot of the SunTrust Bank. The rock building, which is now a Christmas shop, was Waynesville's first library and, before that, a bank.

A special piece of property, lot number eighteen is on the northeast side of Main Street. Jesse Anderson built a storehouse at this location for Robert Love in 1813, and it became Robert Love's home in town. Later owners were C. Kelly, Mrs. L.J. Ratcliff and Alden Howell in 1887. (His ancestor was Joseph Howell who fought in the American Revolution. Alden is buried in Green Hill Cemetery.) A bank was built on this lot. Sara and James Sloan were owners of this bank in 1933 when it went bankrupt. Joe Reinertson then bought the property in 1943 and used this building for an auction house of valuable antiques. The tourists would attend these auctions in the summer. In 1955 Homer and Vergie Justice bought this beautiful old bank building. In 1989 it came into the hands of Nancy Dodd, a collector of antiques, who had plans to restore the building. After her death, it was bought and turned into a nice collection of shops and restaurants called the Towne Square.

Lot number twenty-two is on the northeast side of the street. Robert Love first owned this lot, then James R. Love and later J.M. Tate. By 1921, it was owned by M. Theo and Mary McCracken, who opened a clothing store at the location. There was an outside stairway to an apartment upstairs that remains to this day. Presently, this is the location of the Christian Bible bookstore and other businesses.

Up and across the street, lot number eleven was originally the third lot on the southwest side of the street and was to be an open-air lot for a public market. Like most other things, its function has changed over the years and today it is part of the parking lot of the First Baptist Church. The other part of this

The Shelton House, now a museum, 2006. *Courtesy of Janet Webb.*

parking lot was lot nineteen, although it was originally the house of Samuel Fitzgerald, who built a rock house with a well at the front door.

One of the notable citizens of Waynesville was Dr. J.H. Way, who was born in Waco, Texas, in about 1865. As a young child, his family moved to Asheville. As a young man he studied medicine with a local doctor. Then he went on to Vanderbilt Hospital in Nashville, Tennessee, to finish his education. He was a good, hardworking doctor. He went anywhere, anytime that he was needed. It was an all day trip to Crabtree or Fines Creek. His grandson, Charley Way, said that when he went on a long trip to attend to a patient, he would spend the night with "whoever would put him up." He had two children, J.H. and Hilda. He never retired. He died of pneumonia in 1927.

Some structures on Main Street remain recognizable. It still has a lot of the structures that were here when the street was paved with bricks. But there are some new buildings as well. These have been added as the need has risen.

RICHLAND CREEK AND THE NEARBY COMMUNITIES

People come and go. The lands of Haywood County have witnessed the Indians and the Europeans, the structures they have built and those they have destroyed. But the waterways and the hills and the mountains remain. The rest of the stories in this book are about the ever-present land that is Haywood County.

The bluffs of Richland Creek, 2006. *Courtesy of Janet Webb.*

The ford of Richland Creek with the little Jones Cove Branch entering Richland Creek, 2006. *Courtesy of Janet Webb.*

The headwaters of Richland Creek are in the west part of Haywood County near Balsam Gap. Some of the many tributaries are Winchester Creek, Redbank Branch, Little Branch Creek, Nolen Creek, Drift Branch, Hyatt Creek, Allens Creek, Plott Creek, Eagles Nest Creek, Shelton Creek and Raccoon Creek. Richland Creek flows northeast, passing through Lake Junaluska, until it empties into the Pigeon River below the sewerage plant near Hyder Mountain. The Waynesville Bypass Highway and North Carolina Highway 209 North are close to this creek.

After leaving Balsam Gap, the following landmarks are on either side of Richland Creek: To the north are the Plott Balsams and Eagles Nest Ridge with Little Mountain on the southern shoulder of the ridge. Between the dam at Lake Junaluska and the mouth of Richland Creek to the north are Utah Mountain and the Fincher Mountain. To the south, before Richland Creek bisects Waynesville, is Pinnacle Ridge. After leaving Waynesville, the Ratcliff Mountain rises to the east. Walnut Trail exits from North Carolina Highway 209 across Richland Creek and ends at the sewage treatment plant. Richland Creek curves to its bluffs, and it is low enough to have a ford on the property of the sewage treatment plant. There is an old mill at this part of Richland Creek. The Richland Creek Road exits from North Carolina Highway 209 next to Pigeon River. After a short distance it crosses near the mouth of Richland Creek. The

A 1905 ten-day sale at the Paris Dry Goods Store shortly after Main Street was paved. *Courtesy of the* Enterprise Mountaineer.

road continues for several miles until it connects to the old Asheville/Clyde Highway near the Medford farm area below Woodland Baptist Church.

Old road orders illustrate how these roads came to be. A road order was made in 1809 to build a road from the ford of Richland Creek to the burnt schoolhouse. The burnt schoolhouse may have been on the creek that flows from the hill near Daisy Avenue in Waynesville and empties into Richland Creek near where Church Street ends at Miller Street. This area was close to John Wikle's and Samuel McCabe's homes. The ford of Richland Creek was about two-thirds of a mile from the mouth of Richland Creek, just below the buffs. There are about four curves from the ford to the mouth of Richland Creek on Pigeon River.

A wagon road order was made in 1812 as follows: James Moore was to be an overseer to open a road from the ford on Richland Creek below the bluffs to the forks of the branch above John Howell's house. This was to intersect the road to be laid out from the burnt cabin to Waynesville. Also, Moore was to open a new wagon road from the top of the mountain where it crosses near Captain Stephenson's home. Then he was to join the road that he had surveyed before and go down to the ford below the bluffs on Richland Creek. John Wikle was to be responsible for the care of the road from the ford of Richland Creek to the fork of the road on Jonathan Creek. Those who worked under him lived on the east side of Richland

Creek from the mouth of the creek up to Adam Killian's and John Wikle's homes. More maintenance work was needed on this road in the winter of 1811, and John White was to be the overseer of workers from Oden Killian's place and Edward Hyatt's place, where a man named Bennet Jay lived. The road that derived from this order is now Richland Creek Road from the ford on Richland Creek to North Carolina Highway 209, which intersects U.S. 19 at Lake Junaluska.

Road orders also prescribed improvement on the existing paths and trails. In one early nineteenth-century order, Jonathan Osborn was to be the overseer of a road from the ford on Richland Creek above John Howell's to the camp meeting ground on Shook's Land. The roads that closely follow this layout are the Richland Creek Road and the Old Asheville/Clyde Highway. Some repair work on the road from the public square to Edwards's old storehouse was to be completed above Edward Hyatt's home. This was on the base of Eagles Nest Mountain. Hyatt Creek flows from the side of the mountain and empties into Richland Creek. Houses on this route were the John Welch plantation where Jesse Tolin lived, Robert and Thomas Love's homes, then north to Edward Hyatt's. As the population of the county expanded, so did the orders for wagon roads: more were needed from the James Thompson place to the public square and from James Henson's to Waynesville.

PEOPLE OF RICHLAND CREEK

Many people used the roads on Richland Creek when they were first built. One woman who lived in the area was Mary Magdaline Wigle Tanner. Her last husband was Michael Tanner, although her children were by her first husband. These were John, Michael, Henry, Susannah, George, Elisabeth, Samuel Wigle and Mary Wigle Smith, the wife of Lewis Smith. Mary Magdaline Tanner's will was made on March 15, 1810 and probated in September 1810. Her friend Felix Walker was one of her executors. Lewis Smith and his wife, Mary Wigle Smith, owned 400 acres that he had bought April 17, 1792. These were located on a rocky ridge above Richland Creek and benefited from the addition of new wagon roads. Lewis Smith had bought North Carolina State Grant No. 5, on June 24, 1807, which contained 640 acres on the west side of Richland Creek, next to his old land with an old Indian path close by. This was the place where Edward Hyatt had lived. It was next to the Adam Killian land. Lewis Smith had North Carolina State Grant No. 24 for one hundred acres on September 1809. This new property was next to his land and joined his neighbors' land: Martin Buff, Shadrach Hyatt and John Wikle. On December 16, 1809, Lewis Smith bought North Carolina State Grant No. 11 containing 100 acres. This land included part of the land Osborn had owned. The boundary line ran on the east side of an island in Richland Creek.

Other people who used the roads on Richland Creek were Adam Killian and Thomas C. St. Clair. Adam Killian was well established in the area and owned 302 acres. His home was known as The Kentucky. He sold 5 acres to Thomas

St. Clair, a well-known area citizen, for thirty-five dollars on July 6, 1809. Charles Ellis and Leonard Killian were witness to this deed. Killian's deed was not purchased until February 10, 1810, with Thomas C. St. Clair as a witness.

Robert Love and John Davidson bought North Carolina State Grant No. 970 for 200 acres on Richland Creek on March 21, 1794. This boundary line crossed the creek several times, went up the side of a hill and included a meadow. When Davidson had moved to Franklin County, Tennessee, Robert Love bought the Davidson portion of the land for $300 on October 17, 1809. Robert Love also bought two hundred acres from John Strother for $100 on April 6, 1809. This land was near Chambers's old line on Richland Creek and bordered what was then John Davidson's property on the north side of the creek near a buck yard. Love received North Carolina State Grant No. 1081 on December 22, 1799, for a tract of land but sold 170 acres of this land to John Dillard on July 20, 1811. John Welch sold to Robert and Thomas Love 55½ acres for $600 on June 27, 1809, located where the mouth of Richland Creek enters the Pigeon River. Thomas Love, Robert's brother, and James Brittain owned the land next to Robert Love's now massive acreage. Thomas and Robert Love had bought an additional 5 acres that bordered the millrace near the Brittain line. Holliman Battle was a witness to this deed.

Oxen resting on Main Street in front of the Rogers home after 1904. This is the location of the John Graham Store. *Courtesy of the* Enterprise Mountaineer.

In the many deeds, the currency was listed as dollars, which was the American money, but the British money of shillings and pounds was used as well. The transition time for money to become standard took many years to complete.

James Bird paid the Love brothers $20 for an acre of land on the north bank of Richland Creek on April 3, 1811. James Brittain paid 100 shillings for North Carolina State Grant No. 7, for 200 acres on Richland Creek that included all the vacant land below where Colonel Robert Love lived and adjoined the land that Robert Love bought from Joseph Chambers. Also, Abigail Chambers had a grant for a tract of land on the northwest side of Richland Creek, and her husband, Joseph Chambers, sold 400 acres of it for $550 to John Welch on April 16, 1802. John Fergus and John Colvard were witnesses to this transaction. John Welch also had land adjacent to this acreage and the Chambers's land. This property was a part of the David Allison acres. William Allen and David Messer was a witness to this deed. On the same day John Welch bought 117 acres for $250. This land bordered Joseph Turner, the Chambers family, John Davidson, Thomas Love, John Fergus and John Welch's previous property. William Allen and David Wesner was a witness to this deed. John Welch sold 100 acres to Henry Plott for $300. This fork of Richland Creek was called Dicks Creek. The land was on the north side of the creek next to Isaac's land.

William Welch, the son of John and Dorcas Dillard Welch, was born April 8, 1796 in Virginia. After a two-year trip to Missouri, he returned to Waynesville in 1820. He married his first wife, Martha Love, who only lived a year. He then married her sister, Mary Ann Love, another daughter of Robert Love. William Welch and Mary Ann had ten children. His eight sons all went to college. He gave each son a slave and two horses to use while the son was in college. The eldest son went to Washington College and Transylvania Medical School. During the Civil War, one of the seven sons who served in the Confederacy was killed at the Battle of Piedmont in Virginia. William was a merchant, farmer and hotelier. The couple was active within their community, including the First Baptist Church of Waynesville. In October 1863, Elizabeth Battle made a charge that Mary Ann Welch was guilty of ruling the church. Mary Ann in turn charged Elizabeth with a falsehood. The church decided to solve the conflict by requesting that both women withdraw from the church, but Mary Ann Welch continued to attend. On February 6, 1865, William, who had been in poor health, died; this was during the time that Union Colonel Kirk was making raids through the county. William Welch was buried in Green Hill Cemetery. A few months later his wife, Mary Ann Love Welch, died and was buried beside him in Green Hill Cemetery.

One of the early pioneers, Joseph Dobson, first bought 100 acres on January 10, 1803. This land was near an Indian path and near the wagon road. Several years later, he bought 214 acres on the west fork of Richland Creek on December 17, 1808. This property bordered the William Cathey and the John McDowell farms. Joseph also bought 640 acres, including the place where Martin Buff lived next to the Robert Love property, on December 17, 1808. All of this land is on Richland

Creek. On April 5, 1809, Joseph Dobson bought a quit claim deed of 500 acres on the south side of Pigeon River at the mouth of Richland Creek. This included most of the land where Jonathan Osborn lives. This was adjacent to land owned by Robert Love. Again, Joseph bought another quit claim deed for 640 acres from John Strother of Rutherford, Tennessee on April 14, 1810. He paid one cent for this land. Strother had received it as North Carolina State Grant No. 1728.

Another pioneer was William McConnell, who paid $300 for 100 acres on a branch of the left side of Richland Creek (where Jacob Buff had lived) on November 24, 1807. His witnesses were Martin Buff, Samuel Cabe and William Love. George Buff paid £75 for 100 acres located on the west end of Robert Love's land, near the meadow bottom. The river was one edge of his property. Phil T. Burford and John McAmish were his witnesses to this deed of September 6, 1809. On the same day, his brother Martin Buff bought 640 acres for £150. This property had the river running through it. The deed started on a ridge near Robert Love's line.

The 1903 rock building on Main Street was first a bank, then became the first public library. *Courtesy of the* Enterprise Mountaineer.

The Bryson family was among the pioneers. On August 4, 1803, William Bryson Jr. bought one hundred acres for $50. This was on the trail fork of Richland Creek and the Indian trail adjoining James Bryson's land. His witnesses were James Bryson and Andrew Bryson. On August 24, 1803, James Bryson Sr. received 640 acres on both sides of the trail fork of Richland Creek next to William Bryson's land, for services rendered. His witnesses were William Bryson and Andrew Bryson. On September 20, 1807, Richard Morrow sold 100 acres for $135 to Edward Chasten. This was located at the upper end of William Bryson's land, where someone named Indian John had made some improvements at one time. William Warren and William Allen were witnesses to this deed.

And the lists continue with more courageous people willing to settle in this undeveloped land. John Colbert paid $120 to Henry Inman and Joseph Dobson for some land for Robert Roland on August 20, 1807. Robert received 320 acres on the west fork of Richland Creek above where Edward Hyatt lived as half of a grant to Inman and Dobson. James Stevenson and Solomon Stansbury signed the deed as witnesses. John McDowell received North Carolina State Grant No. 1721 on December 29, 1807. He paid 50 shillings for every 100 acres. His 237 acres were on both sides of Richland Creek, including both of John Morrow's improvements. His neighbors were John Colvard and John Strother. John McDowell also, had land adjoining this property. John McDowell sold this land for $200 to Benjamin Odell Jr. It lies on the small east fork of Richland Creek, next to John Colvard's land on the upper end.

Richland Creek, 2006. *Courtesy of Janet Webb.*

John Fergus and his family came to Buncombe County, which became Scotts Creek, Haywood County, shortly after 1800. John Fergus, a widower married the widowed mother of Holliman Battle. He surveyed some land on Scotts Creek on February 21, 1803, which Holliman Battle eventually sold to Thomas Parton in 1808.

John Howell was born in 1770 and died between 1846 and 1850. In 1803 he bought some land on Richland Creek about six miles from where Waynesville would be, near the mouth of Richland Creek. John Howell and his second wife, Elizabeth Collins Howell, had two daughters. The second daughter, Juliette Howell married Ute Hyatt. John's brother-in-law was Jonathan Osborn. His younger brother, Henry Howell, came to Haywood County in about 1834. Henry's wife was Mary Catherine Miller Howell. He had been widowed a short time before he married Mary.

The Eagles Nest Hotel was built on the edge of Junaluska Mountain around the turn of the century on land almost a mile high. It had a spectacular view of the Richland Creek valley. There were about thirty bedrooms and other public rooms of entertainment and dinning. The water and electricity came from a nearby stream. A road wound up the mountainside from Waynesville to the hotel. Wealthy families would spend the summer. The hotel was burned in 1919 and never rebuilt. Now there are many homes on the side of the mountain, including one built on the old location of the hotel.

East of Waynesville

The People of Raccoon Creek

Raccoon Creek, for the length of its almost five miles, stays a small creek. There are two main tributaries to Raccoon Creek, including the east fork that flows down the valley on the southern side of Ratcliff Mountain. In the hill and valley below Ratcliff Mountain are the homes and orchards of the Franklin, Francis and McCracken families and others. This fork meanders down the hillside to join the west fork of Raccoon Creek beyond where the Raccoon road intersects North Carolina Highway 209 South. The west fork of Raccoon Creek is two-pronged with both branches starting at about one thousand feet on Wolf Pen Mountain. One branch flows down by the Head-Collins property to join the other branch that comes through the Boone, Christopher and other properties. These three tributaries have dozens of small springs. All of this land is in Francis Cove. When the creek becomes the main Raccoon Creek, it winds northeastward beside U.S. Business 23 (part of the way underground in culverts). It joins Richland Creek just before the Hi-Tech Center and the Waynesville Bypass Highway, which is very close to Lake Junaluska.

The mountains that surround Francis Cove on the south are part of the Lickstone Ridge. Two of the closer peaks of this ridge are Beaty Spring Knob and to the west is Wolfpen Mountain with Wolfpen Gap in between. Pigeon Gap (also known as Deaver's Gap, which was referred to in many of the old deeds) separates these peaks from Ratcliff Mountain.

The first road order in 1809 was for a road from the east fork of Raccoon Creek to the burnt cabin. The second road order was from the ford of Raccoon Creek near William Kennady's to the fork of the first branch below James Bryson Jr. The Raccoon Creek Road still follows the creek in a similar path. In the summer of 1809, a maintenance road order was given from the ford of Raccoon Creek by George Cathey's place to the ford of Pigeon River. Jacob Battle was to oversee this work. In 1810 a road was needed from Deaver's Gap on the mountain above Gideon Almon's the public square in Waynesville. It was to continue on to connect with the wagon road at Inman's old store above Edward Hyatt's place. Another order was for a road from Pigeon Gap to a wagon road near Evans's old store near the public square. Then a road was to go on to the Evans stone house above Edward Hyatt's place. Fourth, a road was to start on the branch above Coleman's new house below Pigeon Gap, to go to the public square. To continue the roadwork, Francis Bird was to oversee the road from Pigeon Gap that went to the ford of Pigeon. John Biffle had had this responsibility in the past.

Developing roads in the area made it much easier for folks to build homes in these mountains. Gabriel Ragsdale and Joseph Henry had bought 300 acres of land on the east fork of Raccoon Creek on October 17, 1796. Abraham Shook then bought 100 acres of this land from Ragsdale on September 7, 1805. Finally, John Welch bought land from Philip Burford, whose land joined the Thomas Welch land next to a spring. This land went up the ridge to a point called Isinglass Point (on the side of Wolfpen Mountain) and along the top of the ridge. This land purchase occurred on October 21, 1806.

This was the Garrett Funeral Home next to the First Union National Bank in Waynesville before 1964. *Courtesy of the* Enterprise Mountaineer.

The grand old bank building, 1992. *Courtesy of the* Enterprise Mountaineer.

Laying the cornerstone for the brick courthouse. Colonel Jones's home is in the background, 1882. *Courtesy of the* Enterprise Mountaineer.

On the west fork of the creek, Nathaniel Alman bought 30 acres next to John Dobson and Joseph Turner on October 4, 1809. He sold this land on April 22, 1811 to Gideon Alman. The Crymes Cove road follows the west fork of the creek up a shoulder of Wolfpen Mountain then crosses a gap of the mountain. The Crymes Cove road was named for the Crymes family that lived on the land of the west fork of the creek, near the gap, beginning about 1850.

Macinda Battle, the daughter of William Wayne and Emeline Howell Battle, was born in 1835. When she was thirteen, she climbed a tree to escape a pack of wolves and a man named Ben Hawkins rescued her. She married her first husband, Ben Hawkins, at age fourteen. They had five children. Ben died in the Civil War in 1864, fighting for the Union. Macinda continued to live on the farm on Wolfpen Mountain. In March 1865, the Union officer George Kirk and his troops came to the farm. They burned most of the farm buildings. They tore up things in the home and destroyed or took all the livestock and food they could find. Ben had freed his few slaves before he left for war in 1862, but they chose to remain with Macinda. In 1865, she married William Crymes. She died when she was ninety-nine years of age.

The Boones and Christophers were neighbors of the Crymes family. They all lived on the same side of Wolfpen Mountain near the west fork of Raccoon Creek. The Christophers had a produce market at the foot of this creek. The Christophers

The brick courthouse, Waynesville, 1885. *Courtesy of the* Enterprise Mountaineer.

had farms and an orchard, which produced part of what they sold. The Boones still farm. One of the granddaughters still lives in the old Boone home. It is a brick house located on a hill. One part of the west fork creek flows by this house.

Just below where the forks of the creek join, Thomas Welch bought 150 acres on August 8, 1806. Then, John Welch bought 126 acres next to his brother near the mouth of the creek on February 2, 1809. Mark Coleman Sr. and wife, Margaret, had nine children. One daughter, Sally was "unfortunate" and unable to take care of herself. One daughter, Betsy, was married to Nathaniel Alman and the other daughter, Margaret, was married to Gideon Alman. Their sons were Daniel, John, Jacob, William, Joseph and Mark Coleman, who was married at the time of his father's death in 1818. Mark Coleman Sr. was a German who signed his name Marx Coleman.

William Francis was a millwright from Jonesboro, Tennessee. He came to Haywood County in 1818. In 1820, he married Mary Alman. Her father gave then a nice wedding gift: a farm that was one square mile. The farm boundaries started from the top of Wolfpen Mountain in the north. They went down Raccoon Creek. (This is where the boundary of the mountain research station is now located.) Next to one boundary of the Francis farm was the area called the old schoolhouse, currently the location of the Francis Cove Methodist Church.

The first home they had was a two-room log cabin with a dogtrot between the two rooms. In the 1840s a large white house was built on the property with fireplaces in each room. William Francis started this house and his son, Monteville Pinkney Francis, finished it. It was lived in by Mrs. John Head until 1959. In recent years, the house was destroyed by fire, thought to have been arson. William built his gristmill in 1887 near the east fork of Raccoon Creek. It continued in operation until 1976. This mill has been restored. It can be seen near North Carolina Highway 276. The Francis family still owns the mill.

A famous man was born on Raccoon Creek on February 5, 1805: William Holland Thomas. His mother was widowed just before his birth. She taught Will

Will Thomas, the white chief of the Cherokees, *1880s. Courtesy of the* Enterprise Mountaineer.

at home. In his mid-teens he clerked for Felix Walker near the Indian village. Later, Will and his mother moved into the area close to the Cherokee Indians. As an adult after his adopted father, the Cherokee chief, Will Thomas became the first white chief of the Cherokee People. In the Civil War, he raised a regiment of soldiers to fight for the South. Four companies of these soldiers were Cherokee Indians, the only regiment with Indians in the South. The Sixty-ninth North Carolina Regiment was known as "Thomas' Legion." He was married to Sarah J. Love, the granddaughter of Robert Love. He bought tens of thousands of acres of land in his own name. The Cherokee Indians were to pay him back for the land with money that was to have come from federal payments. Thomas did this because he believed that the Indians should own their own land. During the Civil War, Thomas's business ventures were neglected and he had mounting debts. After the Civil War, his main creditors, William Johnston and sons, foreclosed and Will Thomas's lands were auctioned. The Cherokee Indians sued Thomas for neglect of trust because their homeland was in danger of being taken away from them. Thomas was very sympathetic to the Indians. He said in arbitration that the land should belong to the Cherokee Indians. Thus, today there is a homeland for the Eastern Band of the Cherokee Indians. William died in 1893 at the state home for the insane in Morganton, North Carolina.

THE PEOPLE OF THE FLOWERY GARDENS AND CENTER PIGEON

The Flowery Gardens was located in the area just north of Bethel on North Carolina Highway 110. This was below where the east fork and the west fork of the Pigeon River join in the Center Pigeon area. John McDowell may have named this area, for he had lived in Pleasant Garden, Burke County, North Carolina. This area is not known as the Flowery Gardens today, but there is a road marker identifying this former location. Ratcliff Mountain and Anderson Mountain are to the north and Cold Mountain is to the south of this little valley. The area is limited as to where roads could be located because the valley is narrow. The river is close to the road.

William Mahaffy was the overseer in June 1809 of some roadwork that started at the forks of a road that went from the head of Hominy Creek to the ford of Pigeon River. This began at the place of John Leiper and went south to the Garden Creek area.

Although there had previously been some Indian settlements in this area, among the first Europeans who arrived in Flowery Gardens were Jonathan McPeters and David Nelson, his indentured servant. They made a crop in about 1785 and left after it was harvested. John and Joseph McDowell bought North Carolina State Grant No. 1265 on November 27, 1789, about three miles down the river below where Rutherford's army crossed. This particular area in 1789 was Burke County and changed to Buncombe County in 1791. However, it was finally included with the creation of Haywood County in 1808. On August 17, 1809, the sheriff of

Buncombe County sold some land for John McDowell Jr. from the legatees of the estate of John McDowell Sr., deceased. John McDowell Sr. had a title to some land in the Flowery Gardens on April 17, 1792. He also had purchased North Carolina State Grant No. 8 for one hundred acres on January 21, 1795. Later, Jonathan Plott bought this land in 1830. There is a large home on this land. The roadside marker states that it was once the Plott home.

Mathias Mease was the next of several families to settle in the area of Flowery Gardens. He bought 200 acres in Flowery Gardens on March 14, 1807. His land bordered a Mr. Barret's land on one side of the creek and Adam Killian's land on the other side of the creek. George Strother and Robert Gillespie were witnesses to this deed. Another in the same area, David McPeters bought 150¾ acres of land on the Pigeon River next to Killian. This purchase occurred on April 10, 1809, with James B. Love as a witness. Finally, Thomas Foster Jr. and Elihu Chamber bought fifty acres of land on the west side of Pigeon River opposite Flowery Gardens for $125 on October 8, 1811, from Joseph Sorrels. This was next to the plantation where Elihu Chambers lived. Joshua Kinworthy was a witness to this deed for Joseph Sorrels, but his wife Sarah Kinworthy acknowledged the deed in court for Thomas Foster Jr.

Jonathan Osborne made a will March 26, 1805, but he lived until 1828. He had property in the Flowery Gardens. His three sons were Roland, Sherod and Ephraim. Roland was an administrator of his father's estate. Also, he set some of his slaves free in his will.

BETHEL AND PETER COVE BRANCH

The Bethel community is an open valley. To the west, the mountains Beaty Spring Knob and Round Knob descend from Lickstone Ridge. The mountain to the south is Cold Mountain, which is part of the Great Balsam Mountains. To the north are Ratcliff Mountain, Pressley Mountain and Rocky Knob and to the east is Poison Cove Top Mountain. The West Fork of Pigeon River is the main north-south waterway in this area. Peter Cove Branch and Bird Creek are tributaries of the west fork in Bethel. In the eastern part of the valley Dix Creek joins East Fork of Pigeon River as it makes a brief appearance before joining the West Fork and becoming the head of Pigeon River, in a community known as Woodrow. Another area nearby is Center Pigeon, formerly known as Flowery Gardens. Starting in the north and going clockwise are the following mountainside coves: Poison Cove, Chambers Cove, Edward Cove and Peter Cove to the north. U.S. 276 East stretches from Waynesville into Francis Cove, through Pigeon Gap, then winds down the mountain through Bethel, up the East Fork of the Pigeon River and across the mountain into the next county. There is a road going south up the West Fork. This road going north from Bethel is the old road, North Carolina Highway 215, on the west side of Pigeon River going to Canton. Beginning at a traffic light on the eastern end of Bethel on

U.S. Highway 276, North Carolina Highway 110 goes north to Canton through Center Pigeon, a northern branch of the Bethel valley.

Elijah Deaver was to oversee a road from Pigeon Gap to the ford of Pigeon River. This route appears to have been from the gap between Wolf Pen Mountain and Ratcliff Mountain down the mountain through Bethel, turning north up Pigeon River on what would become North Carolina Highway 215 to Canton. Deaver was also in charge of road maintenance on the road from Davis Ford on Pigeon River to the gap of the mountain.

There are some unusual places and things in the Bethel area. First there was a bridge across the Pigeon River near Bethel. It was a truss bridge, built in 1891. This was the oldest working bridge in North Carolina. Second is the old county home, an early attempt at caring for needy people run by W.L. Moody. This was right after the Civil War and lasted until nearly 1884. The county sold that land in Dellwood and bought 140 acres of the Blaylock farm, where they built a county home in 1912. It was a large brick house. Poor families that could not provide for themselves, orphans, and old people who had no one to care for them all lived here. In the late 1930s the children were taken from the home and placed in foster homes or put up for adoption. In March 1955, the home was closed. The last residents were moved to nursing homes. The county home building was sold and is now part of the Pigeon Valley Rest Home.

Mr. Logan owned the first Model T Ford in Waynesville. He became a dealer for the Ford Motor Company, circa 1910. *Courtesy of the* Enterprise Mountaineer.

Joseph Turner Cathey started this house before the Civil War and completed it in 1864. This is on Highway 276 south before entering Bethel. *Courtesy of Janet Webb.*

Joseph Cathey was educated at home, as there were no private schools in the area. A self-educated man, he had abilities in business and was also a farmer, merchant, miller, trader and family physician. Cathey was an excellent legislator. He knew law, theology, medicine and physics. Cathey was a member of the Methodist Church. He was born March 12, 1803, the only child of William B. and Catherine Turner Cathey. Joseph Cathey married Nancy Alice Hyatt on March 24, 1825. They had nine children born between 1826 and 1845. Joseph died on June 1, 1874.

In 1848, Joseph Cathey received a letter that notified him that he had been nominated for a public office. The letter does not say what the office was. This letter came back into the Cathey family by way of an antique dealer from Canton, who had bought the letter in Tennessee. This was 155 years after Joseph Cathey first received the letter. The house that the Tom Cathey family now lives in is the 1864 house. This was the house that the son of Joseph and Nancy, Joseph Turner Cathey, started to build in 1860, but he was unfortunately killed in the Civil War.

Pigeon River

This river begins at Bethel and continues to Canton. This was the location referred to as the ford of Pigeon River, the crossing for the original Warpath. After leaving Canton and flowing through Clyde, the river turns north between Chambers Mountain on the west and Utah Mountain on the east. It flows crookedly among Hazel Top, White Oak and Longarm Mountains on the west and Cedar Cliff, Oak Knob, Hurricane Mountain and Snowbird Mountain on the east. The Pigeon River leaves North Carolina from the gorge beside Interstate 40 and joins French Broad River at Newport, Tennessee.

On the east side of the Pigeon River was one of the prime areas where many people settled. The first person was John Bellah, who gave $40 to James Stiles for 10½ acres in this area on February 20, 1806. James and Thomas Stiles owned plenty of land on this northeast location. In the same area, Spencer Rice sold 163 acres, including an island in the Pigeon River, to James Leeser for $1,500 on February 5, 1807. Leeser's neighbors were William and Joseph England, William Cathey and the Mahaffeys. On February 10, 1809, John McFarland spent $300 for 150 acres on the east side of Pigeon River that bordered the land of John Fulbright. On the same day he paid $400 for 75 acres next to Joseph Dobson's land and Michael Defadeller's old line. William Stodghel also occupied this area, buying 130 acres on the east side of Pigeon River for $270 on December 26, 1809. This deed started in a cove of a mountain near Defadeller's line. The boundary line was next to William Burris's property, Shook's Land and David Killian's land, also bordering the Will Shoal Branch. Fergus also owned some land in the area next to John and William Stiles. He sold 50 acres of this land to Robert Dickey on March 26, 1810. Finally, George Buff sold 450 acres to Jonathan Osborn on March 17, 1811. This was next to John Bellah's land and near the old Joseph Dobson survey. Finally, William Mahaffey bought 170 acres from the State of North Carolina on October 8, 1810. Alexander Staret McClure and Samuel Hughes signed the deed as witnesses.

The west side of the area also contained good land in the early days of Haywood County. Men began to purchase this farming land, beginning with Obediah Bradshaw, who bought 100 acres from David McDowell on December 2, 1806. This land joined the land of James McDowell and bordered a hill. Two years later, Benjamin Hide paid $25 for 100 acres on March 8, 1808. And on October 24, 1808, Nathaniel Alman sold 100 acres to Robert Martin. This was on the west side of the Edward Pybrun land. After the county was formed, on June 17, 1811, the next three men bought land on Pigeon River: John Robinson bought 37½ acres for twenty five dollars and Robert Phillips bought ninety acres for $75. On June 17, 1811, Jesse Owens bought 199 acres for $200. Then, Stephen William moved next to the Rosses and McDowells when he paid $25.59 for 76½ acres on Pigeon River. Finally, William Williams became Obediah Bradshaw's neighbor in October 1811, when he bought 100 acres on Pigeon

River and McMullins Creek. Also, James Bradshaw had a plantation on the Pigeon River and bought additional land from William McDowell. This was north of the Obediah Bradshaw place. Thomas Bird bought a quit claim on November 30, 1809, to land on which Nathan, Elijah and Richard Deaver had once lived. George Davidson had a common boundary with this property. Joseph Dobson, who had a quit claim on this same acreage, signed a release on September 6, 1809 for 500 acres, less 100 acres, which was sold to Lebanon Nix for $114 on October 17, 1810, where P. McClure lived at the time of the purchase. This tract was next to George Shuler, and Henry Plott bought additional land in the area in 1810.

The next men in 1811 to secure land on Pigeon River were John Massey and Elihu Church. Lastly, the man who purchased land in 1811 was John Dillard who bought one hundred acres. This land was adjacent to the Robert Love two-hundred-acre land grant of July 29, 1811.

SHOOK'S LAND AND CLYDE TOWNSHIP

Jacob Shook came to Haywood County around 1786 after having served in the American Revolutionary War. Jacob's name in German was Vater Shuck. The house that Jacob built in about 1795 started out as a log house. An attic room in the house eventually became a chapel thirty feet long, eighteen feet wide and nine feet high. This was where Bishop Francis Asbury is supposed to have preached in 1810. In 1840, Shook sold the house to William Welch. Then in 1850 the house was transferred to Levi Smathers. Then Levi doubled the size of the house and put clapboard siding over the sawmill siding. It was at this time that the large porches were added to the house. Joseph Hall, a descendent of Jacob Shook, bought the house. He has restored it and turned it into a museum. This is possibly the oldest house in Haywood County.

Clyde lies on the south side of the Pigeon River. On the north side of the river is Interstate 40. There was a path that ran from Newfound Creek on the Buncombe County line to the Indian nation. It followed the south side of the Pigeon River from the ford in Canton through the Clyde area. The river crossed through Clyde at Deaver's Ford, near the route of the Old Asheville Highway. The Clyde Township was formed in 1877, and train rails entered in 1883. J.M. Shook had owned the property on which the depot was built. Then in 1889 Clyde was incorporated. The boundary of the town of Clyde is a circle. It is said that the knothole in a flood board of the train station was the key point from which the boundaries of the town were drawn.

Clyde was a central location for joining the eastern and western parts of the county. In the early days of Haywood County, the Loves and others owned land at the mouth of Richland Creek. They needed a way to get to Shook's Land. The first road order was given in the March 1809 court for a road to be built from the protracting ground near Jacob Shook's land to the ford of Richland Creek. Workers for this road in 1809 lived below George Cathey's, down the river to the mouth of

Richland Creek where it empties into the Pigeon River across from Stillhouse Gap. The Pigeon River then makes a curve around the foot of Hyder Mountain. Two years later, in 1811, it was time to do some maintenance work on this road. Jonathan Osborn was to be overseer of the road from the camp meeting ground on Shook's branch to the ford of Richland Creek above John Howell's home. The names of the men and their employees that were responsible for this work were so ordered: the workers of George Cathey Sr. were to do the work on the west side and up the south side of the creek and out to the mountain. James Chambers, Thomas Welch, Thomas Stiles, John Dillard, Abraham Hannah, Samuel Cabe, Jonathan Gaddy and Joseph Starkey also provided workers for this project.

The direction of this route may have been on the old Asheville Highway, west from Clyde until passing the Medford Cemetery before turning north on Richland Creek Road and following the Pigeon River until it intersects with North Carolina Highway 209 North. The ford on Richland Creek is on the property of the sewage treatment plant on North Carolina Highway 209.

In 1810, a wagon road was needed from the road at Eaton's near George Cathey's meadow to the Haywood County Courthouse that was to be erected near Robert Love's home. This may have been the route of the old Asheville Road. By the winter of 1811, work was needed on a road in the Clyde area; John L. Ford was to be the overseer and it was to run from the fork of the road above George Cathey Jr.'s property to the top of the ridge above Jacob Shook's place. In yet another work order, Daniel Eaton was to oversee the road from the Warpath Ford of Pigeon on to the camp meeting ground above the Deaver house. This road had gone past the Alexander's plantation, Widow Chambers' plantation and Jacob Shook's on the north side of the river from Clark Branch to Crabtree Mountain. William Henderson was to oversee the work on the road from the ford of Pigeon River at William Henderson's to the camp meeting ground near Jacob Shook's home.

The information in the deed book recorded the settlement of this low valley. On January 10, 1803, Joseph Dobson bought four hundred acres next to Shook's land on both sides of Shook Creek. Then on November 21, 1808 Joseph Dobson sold to Jacob Shook two hundred acres for $450, and the land became known as Deaver's Ford. Joseph Dobson had bought this land from Joshua William on October 7, 1804. The North Carolina State Grant was given to Joshua William on July 7, 1794.

Joseph Henry bought one hundred acres on February 6, 1808, on the West Side of the Pigeon River above Deaver's Ford. The land ran on both sides of a branch of the north fork of the first creek that runs into Pigeon River, including Sugar Tree Cove and joining Widow Chambers's land. He paid one hundred dollars to James Buist. His witnesses were John Woode, Robert Gillespie and Robert Love.

On December 26, 1809, William Stoghel bought 130 acres on the East Side of the Pigeon River including part of a cove on the mountain. This land had common boundaries with Michael Defadellar, William Burris, Will Shoal, David Killian and the Shooks. Three days later, Jonathan Woodde bought 75 acres next to Michael Defadellar.

A very old house in Clyde, late 1800s. *Courtesy of the* Enterprise Mountaineer.

The oldest house in Haywood County in located in Clyde. It was built by Jacob Shook, with an addition and remodeling by his son. Today it has been restored and is a museum. *Courtesy of the* Enterprise Mountaineer.

The death records give an insight into the lives of these folks. After John Shook died, the inventory of estate was filed on March 1810. It appears that everything was to be sold. Even Shook's widow, Mary, had to buy the things that she wanted or needed in her home: one hen pot, one hand ax, one weeding hoe, one dresser and furniture, one bay mare and saddle and bridle, one bell and collar, two cows with bells and collar, six chairs, one feather bed and furniture, one half bushel container, one loom, three sheep, stack of hay, one sofa, one flax wheel, two sows and pigs and two hogsheads. When all household goods, farm goods, pigs, horses, cattle and sheep were sold, the money received was over $700. This money became the estate that was divided among the heirs of John Shook. It was a large amount in 1810! Abraham Shook bought one pair of John's shoes. Jacob Shook was one of the administrators of John's estate.

George Cathey willed that his still and vessels were to be sold. This money and the money from debts due him were to be applied to what he owed after his death. He named his wife, Sarah, and his son Spencer, who was under twenty-one years of age at the time Cathey wrote this will June 2, 1828. There were other minor children living with his wife. Some of the names of his children in addition to Spencer (1808) are William (1805), Selena Elizabeth (1806), James N. (1812), Byers (1819) and Lucinda (1825). He had about nine children. He died August 17, 1828. Sarah died before 1860 and she had never remarried.

Pigeon River and Canton

Located in a bend of the river near an island called the Warpath Ford of Pigeon River, there were only two homes in 1861, as this was farmland and swampland, although there was a post office with Robert Penland as postmaster. By 1881 the railroad ended at this location and a train station was built. It was two years before the rails were extended farther west and a few more homes were added to this new railroad village. By an act of the legislature in 1889, the village's name officially became Pigeon River.

Receiving its name in 1895, Canton has since been a paper mill town. It is a place of many hills, some very steep. Originally, the Warpath ran through this location and forded the Pigeon River near a small island close to a big curve in the river. Pigeon River is not a very large river, but it has many pretty areas along the basin of the waterway, and the area around Canton is no exception. Chambers Mountain to the northwest is one of the higher mountains in the area and has been the site of a lookout fire tower for many years. To the north, the Newfound Mountain borders Buncombe County, connected to Chambers Mountain by Glade Mountain, another high mountain in the area. Newfound Mountain connects to Holland Mountain via Newfound Gap. Beaverdam Creek heads in Glade Mountain and empties into the Pigeon River in northern Canton. To the southwest of Canton are Thompson Knob, Spring Hill and Sugar Top Mountains. Crossing the valley formed where the east fork and west fork join to make Pigeon River is Anderson Mountain to the south of Canton. This was a nice farming valley for the people who first came to that area.

One of the old roads leading toward Buncombe County was the Newfound Road. After crossing the ford of Pigeon River, this road turned northeast to follow the North Hominy Creek, crossed the Newfound Gap and entered Buncombe County. Another old road was built along Hominy Creek to the east of Canton. Much later it became a three-lane road designated as U.S. 19-23-74 East. Finally, Interstate 40 passes through Canton, following the Thickety and Beaverdam Valleys. After passing Canton, the road cuts along the south shoulder of Holland Mountain and enters Buncombe County close to where the three-lane road enters. Shortly after entering Buncombe County, there is a cloverleaf connector for these two roads.

In the March court of 1809, a road order was given to make a road from the border of Buncombe County at Jesse Bettoor's property to the ford of Pigeon River at the William Haynes place. This became either Hominy Creek Road or Newfound Road. George Cathey Sr. was to oversee the work on another road leading from the lower side of Osborn's bottoms to the ford of the Pigeon River above William Chambers to the Richland Road beyond the George Cathey place. Alexander had a home near the ford on Pigeon River. A road was to start there and go to the top of the mountain at the head of Newfound. A wagon road was needed starting from Alexander's at the ford to go to the burnt cabin, also known as Mount Prospect

Many people came early to this good land. Of the people who lived in this area, James Chambers was living on a grant of land until he died in 1790. Then Joseph Dobson purchased 640 acres on the west side of Pigeon River including the place where James Chambers lived in his lifetime. This deed was dated January 10, 1803. It was for 500 acres including George Buff's place, next to Robertson and Love's properties. The next men to get grants were George and Thomas Davidson, who acquired North Carolina State Grant No. 45 for 300 acres on the west side of Pigeon River. This was near a hill and included the old Indian Field near the Warpath Ford. The survey set the boundaries on the bank of the river near an island next to James McNabb's land. This was dated January 9, 1794. Next to arrive were John Davidson and David Allison, who both had land in 1796. The last of the arrivals of the eighteenth century was Robert Martin, who received land in 1798. After the turn of that century, William Alexander lived on a branch of the river as a neighbor to John Crage. A wagon road was to be marked out going from Alexander's ford to the burnt cabin, otherwise, Mount Prospect. This was ordered in the September 1811 court session. John Crage sold his land to Isaac Eaton, who later sold some of it to brothers Daniel and Jesse Eaton on March 1, 1810. On October 6, 1810, Daniel Eaton sold his brother his land. Other big landowners in the early nineteenth century were George Hall, James Abel and John McFarland.

Other people of interest were the Reverend William Haynes and his wife, Elizabeth, daughter of Allen Hood. They had a son, Humphrey Posey Haynes. Humphrey was born August 4, 1824. Also, Robert Penland who was postmaster of Pigeon River in 1861.

The John Curtis Store in Canton, mid 1900s. *Courtesy of the* Enterprise Mountaineer.

Oxen were used to move logs to the paper mill in Canton, early 1900s. *Courtesy of the* Enterprise Mountaineer.

Canton's Main Street looking west in 1910. *Courtesy of the* Enterprise Mountaineer.

The old Warpath Ford at Canton, 1895. *Courtesy of the* Enterprise Mountaineer.

DUTCH COVE

Dutch Cove is a small valley community to the southwest of Canton that is located on the Dutch Cove Creek. This creek flows in a northwesterly direction into Hominy Creek near Canton. The Pisgah National Forest is on the south and Chestnut Mountain is to the northeast.

An interesting man that lived in this area was Christian Sergeant Messer, who came here in 1796. He was born before 1770. After living in Dutch Cove for a while, he moved to the Panther Creek section of Fines Creek. His son Fed was born in 1791 according to one story, although the 1850 census reported the birth date as 1793 and he died in 1907. When Fed was about thirty years old, he married Anna Hunter on October 17, 1828. She was about thirteen years old. She died in 1894. They had a large family. In 1850 the children were listed as Jackson (about twenty-one years of age); Adra, a daughter (about twenty); Samuel (about seventeen) and C.F., a son (about sixteen). These older children may have died before 1860. Next was Marisa, who was born about 1836. She was not in the 1880 census. The next boy, Conrad, born in 1838, married before 1860. He was gone from the census records by 1870 and may have been a casualty of the Civil War. The last daughter was Susannah J., born September 1860, who lived with her father in 1900. She was living by herself in 1910, age forty-nine. Richard John was born about 1845. He was with his family in 1850 through 1870. The 1900 census reported that Fed was a widower who had fathered seven children, although only two of them were still living. The 1900 census also gave Fed's birth date as August 1798. If this is true, Fed Messer was 109 when he died!

More Messers were George W. Messer born in 1797 and Christian Jack Messer who was close to George's age. John Messer and Thomas Solomon Messer were born around 1800. David Messer and Joseph Messer were the youngest of the Messer men. Old Solomon Messer died in 1825. Solomon and Rachel had a large number of children. Sally Gibson, Jane Harrison, Elizabeth Cline and Amy Crawford were their married daughters. The rest of their children are Joseph, Peggy, Solomon, John, Rachel, Henry, Ruben and Polly.

Benjamin Brookshire, who sold some land, made his mark on the deed. It is said that the Brookshires who first arrived in Haywood County lived in the hollow of a large chestnut tree until their cabin was built. During the time of sleeping in the tree, his wife gave birth to their son! They later returned to Buncombe County.

Fed Messer, who was born in 1791 and died 1908. *Courtesy of the* Enterprise Mountaineer.

BEAVERDAM, HOMINY AND NORTH HOMINY

Beaverdam is a long valley (a little over three miles) on the north side of Canton. The Newfound Mountain is at the head of Beaverdam Creek. Starting with the first mountain on the west is Sassafras Ridge, then Buck Cove Mountain and Rocky Knob. On the east are the hills and mountains of Little Piney Top, Sidney Top, Williams Mountain and Doubleside Knob. Rice Cove, West Cove and Wilson Cove all open onto the Beaverdam valley. Beaverdam Road strays from Newfound Road up to the center of the valley to Beaverdam Gap. The layout of a wagon road, starting from Benjamin Clark's home on Beaverdam and continuing on to William Chambers's home, was ordered in the fall of 1812.

Because of the early settlers in this area, Beaverdam became one of the original precincts in the county. Hezekiah Allen sold 50 acres next to Isaac Eaton's land to David McPeter on Beaverdam Creek on October 3, 1800. John Strother sold a tract of land to Isaac Robinson Sr. on March 23, 1805. Isaac Robinson Sr. sold 150 acres of this tract to his son Isaac Robinson Jr. for $50 on June 24, 1809. He also sold another 100 acres to John Robinson for $50. Both of these tracts of land had the Beaverdam Creek running through them. William Gillespie bought 209 acres from Isaac Robinson for $500 on September 22, 1809. Benjamin Clark and William Robinson were his neighbors. William Eaton bought 60 acres next to the Smith place on October 14, 1807.

Some men waited until the last days of their lives to write wills. William Gillespie was one such person. He wrote his will on April 8, 1811 and it was probated in the June Session of Court, 1811. In it he named his wife, Susannah, and sons, James C. Gillespie and William Gillespie, as heirs. His daughters were Mary, Jean, Malinda and Matilda. He lived next to John Fulbright. The three witnesses to his will were John McFarland, Benjamin Black and William Clark. Taylor Gillespie and John Fulbright qualified as executors of the last will and testament of William Gillespie, deceased. Susannah Gillespie assisted in the sales and inventory of this estate.

Newfound Road travels along North Hominy and this road enters Buncombe County at Newfound Gap. Between North Hominy and Hominy is Holland Mountain. Hominy, a narrow valley along the Holland Creek, is to the east of Canton. There was a turnpike built in this valley for the purpose of entering Buncombe County. Chestnut Mountain is to the south. This mountain separates Hominy from Dutch Cove. In 1809, a road order was given to mark out a road on Hominy Creek from Spivey's old place to the mouth of Spruce Pine Branch above Daniel Flemming's property.

An order was also given to make a road from the Buncombe County line on Hominy Creek near Jesse Ballen's to the banks of the road above Daniel Flemming's. Ehilu Chambers became the one to oversee the road from the forks of the road at Hominy Creek to the Warpath Ford of the Pigeon River in 1810. James Leiper was charged as an overseer of the work on the road from the forks of the road at the head of Hominy to the ford of the river above James Leiper's place in the winter of

1811. Then a year later, James Leiper was the overseer of the road from the forks of the road at the head of Hominy to the ford of the river above the Suser's property. The workers from John Massey's and Elihu Chambers and the ones on the Flowery Garden Creek were to work for James Leiper. Elihu Chambers was a noted surveyor and was reported to be a very large man, tall and strong.

Jacob Evans sold 50 acres to John Fulbright for $300 on May 18, 1811. This part of Hominy Creek was known as Thompsons Mill Fork. Nathan Thompson and Jacob Shook was witness to this deed. Thomas C. St. Clair paid $320 for 640 acres on December 1811. This land was on the North Fork of Hominy Creek. His neighbors were George Hall and Colonel Daniel Smith.

WEST FORK OF PIGEON RIVER AND LAKE LOGAN WAY

The west fork of the Pigeon River rises near the top of the mountains between Fork Mountain and Fork Ridge near the Haywood County and Transylvania County line. Most of the valley of the west fork is narrow until it gets close to Bethel, although it widens at Cecil. A little farther down the mountain is Riverside, which has several farms. The land here opens up into the valley where Bethel lies. Most of the people in this area do not now depend on farming. The little east fork joins the west fork at Cecil. Lickstone Ridge is the large mountain to the west, and Fork Mountain again separates the west fork and the little east fork. At the lower end of Fork Mountain is Cecil. On the road that follows the west fork, Inman Chapel is to the west of the road. A short distance up the mountain is Lake Logan. Champion Paper Mill Company developed this man-made lake from a reservoir in 1931. Before the lake was built, it was a logging camp that burned in 1925. Several different groups, including the Episcopal Church (which uses their part of the property as a place of retreat), now own the lake. The road up the river goes to the Blue Ridge Parkway. The tributaries are Queen Creek, Laurel Branch, Curtis Cove Creek and Hickory Flat Cove Creek. Burnett Siding Church is near the mouth of Curtis Cove Creek on the opposite side of the River. Sunburst is at the upper end of Lake Logan. This was another logging camp in the early history of the paper mill. Below Lake Logan are McClure Creek, Sam Branch, Poplar Branch and Inman Branch. This last creek heads up on Beaty Spring Knob. The coves are Edwards Cove and Chambers Cove. On the little east fork is Daniel Boone Camp for Boy Scouts, near the Shining Rock Wilderness Area of the Smokies and the Blue Ridge Parkway. On the east is Cold Mountain.

Nathan Deaver received $1,000 for one hundred acres from Thomas Bird on September 5, 1809, which bordered the lands of his brothers, Elijah and William Deaver. The witnesses to this deed were Jonathan and Margaret Bird. On this same day William Deaver received $300 from Thomas Bird on a quit claim for twenty or thirty acres.

Ninian Edmonston was born in what became Buncombe County while it was still Burke County, on October 21, 1789. While he was very young, his family moved to the west fork of Pigeon River. Edmonston was educated at home, as there were no private schools in the area. He excelled in having a logical mind and in mathematics. He became a surveyor and later served in the War of 1812. He was sheriff of the county, then two terms as chief executive officer of the county. Edmonston joined the Baptist Church. He married Mary Ann Strother on January 14, 1823, a woman fifteen years younger than he. From 1821 through 1836 he was elected to serve in the house and senate in Raleigh. He was a successful farmer and left a lot of property when he died in 1868. The Edmonston children were Rufus A. (born 1826), Laura C. (1831), Dorothy T. (1834), Benjamin F. (1837), Nancy A. (1843), and Thomas B. (1845). Ninian Edmonston died when he was seventy-nine.

Mrs. Bright's boardinghouse on Main Street in 1879. *Courtesy of the* Enterprise Mountaineer.

This home built in the early 1900s by Henry Francis is located on Crymes Cove Road. *Courtesy of Janet Webb.*

EAST FORK OF PIGEON RIVER AND CRUSO

The east fork of the Pigeon River starts on the top of the mountain in the Shining Rock Wilderness Area. This is on the Blue Ridge Parkway on the county line, next to Transylvania County. Cold Mountain is to the west and Pisgah Mountain and Pisgah Ridge lie to the east. Also on this ridge is the Buncombe County line. Some of the land names to the east are Beech Knob, Fryingpan Mountain (where a lookout fire tower is located), Fryingpan Gap, Big Bald, Piney Field Top, Fork Mountain, Mount Pisgah (where the TV tower for WLOS-TV is located) and Rocky Face Mountain. To the north are Sugar Top and Poison Cove Top Mountains. West of the east fork of Pigeon River are Roland Ridge and Cold Mountain. Some of the tributaries of east fork are Ugly Creek, Bee Branch, Crawford Creek and Hungry Creek. Below Cruso is Chinquapin Creek that joins Pisgah Creek before it enters the creek of the east fork. Some more little waterways are Cold Creek, Long Branch and Harley Branch. Next Burnett Creek comes down Burnett Cove to enter east fork. Then there is Lenior Creek before Dix Creek, on which the Mount Zion church is located. There are many churches on the East Fork River as well as land suitable for farms. Several years ago a sign was erected on the road that travels to Cruso. It said, "Nine miles of friendly people and one old grouch." The people of

Cruso take great pride in this joke. They even have an annual contest to elect the "old grouch." Despite this title, the people of Cruso are really a very friendly group of folks.

In 1809 the road from the upper plantation on the east fork of Pigeon River down the creek was to have maintenance under the overseer, Thomas Lenoir. In 1810 there was an order to build a wagon road starting near the property of John McFarland, Esquire, and going to the public square in Waynesville.

John Bellah lived on seventy acres in the area before he bought it from Spencer Rice on August 4, 1803. His neighbors were Spencer Rice, William Cathey Jr. and the Mehaffeys. James Leeser and Robert Jones were witnesses to this deed. Five years later, John McFarland bought 160 acres on April 5, 1808. His land joined William Cathey, Elijah Deaver and the McPeter place. John McFarland owned several large tracts of land. He was four years a senator to the General Assembly of North Carolina. The next year, North Carolina State Grant No. 6 was issued to Robert Henry for two hundred acres on the upper side of John McFarland's land. Elihu Chambers and his helpers surveyed this land on December 20, 1809. One of the many land speculations for Robert Love was on September 30, 1809. Robert Love had purchased the Joseph Dobson four-hundred-acre surveys by a quit claim deed at a sheriff sale, and it had a patent date of December 7, 1803. It was above the Robert Road's tract, which became George Cathey's. This acreage included the old Penland place. Later, Robert Love sold it to Peter Penland on September 29, 1810.

Thomas Lenoir moved into Haywood County in 1799. Lenoir farmed, raised cattle and owned a large number of slaves. After more than thirty years, Lenoir went back to Wilkes County. One of his sons came to his property to manage it.

West of Waynesville

Dellwood

Dellwood is the land between Jonathan Creek and Lake Junaluska. On Lake Junaluska is the assembly for the United Methodist Church, the Southeast Jurisdiction. The community of Dellwood extends from where Lake Junaluska intersects U.S.-19 to the intersection of Jonathan Creek road. Fractor Branch starts in Dellwood and goes down the slope to empty into Lake Junaluska on the western edge of the lake. Before the lake was built in 1913, the creek would have gone into Richland Creek before it entered the narrows. The narrows is the place where the footbridge crosses the lake as part of a walking path.

Across Hard Ridge to the south is Mauney Cove. To the north is Utah Mountain. A shoulder of this mountain is known as Ad Tate Knob. A terrible and sad crime was committed in a cave on this knob in the early 1900s. A woman known only as Nancy took her small granddaughter and put her in a small cave on Tate Knob. She closed up the opening and left the child to die. Later, some men who had formed a search party discovered the body of the child. The criminal, Nancy, spent many years in the state prison for women.

Edward Hyatt, born in England, came to this county by way of Maryland. When he came to western North Carolina with two of his sons, they first went to the Pigeon River near the Warpath Ford. They did not care for that area and finally settled in Dellwood. Edward Hyatt used a mark (X) for his name, suggesting that either he was illiterate or he used this as his official identification mark. His wife's name was Hannah (born 1775). She was the daughter of Edward Leatherwood (1754–1808) and Elizabeth (Quatie) Walker. Elizabeth was a Cherokee Indian. Their sons were Shadrack, Elisha, Nathan and Able. Their daughters were Alsi (the wife of William Allen) and Airy (wife of Joseph Young). Hyatt had slaves, including a young girl named Celi, the oldest child another slave woman. The will was made on February 6, 1817. At the time he made his will, his son Nathan was living in the Indian lands. When Edward died, he was at the home of one of his sons.

Left: Alden Howell House on Main Street, Waynesville, 1890s. *Courtesy of the* Enterprise Mountaineer.

Below: Before 1902, Main Street, Waynesville. *Courtesy of the* Enterprise Mountaineer.

The People of Scotts Creek

Hyatt Creek is on the north and Allens Creek is on the south of South Main Street as it leaves Waynesville to the west. After exiting Waynesville, the town street joins U.S. Highway 74-23, then on to Balsam Gap on the Jackson County line. Little Mountain is between Hyatt Creek and the highway next to Richland Creek. On the south of the highway is Pinnacle Ridge. On the other side of Pinnacle Ridge is Big Cove that opens onto Allens Creek. At Balsam Gap is an entrance to the Blue Ridge Parkway. After crossing Balsam Gap the road follows Scotts Creek down the mountain. Judaculla Mountain is on the south side of the highway and Scotts Creek. The next place westward is the town of Sylva.

Judaculla Rock is located on the Caney Fork Road. This is off North Carolina Highway 107, between Cullowhee and Glenville. This is a large soapstone rock. It has carvings of a strange appearance. The markings look like stick figures or even some kind of writing. So far no one has been able to explain what the markings mean or who made them. The Cherokee people named the rock after a Cherokee monster. This monster lived in a cave at Devil's Courthouse, a high rocky overlook on the Blue Ridge Parkway. There are no other rocks with markings like this in the area. Archaeologists think that the rock is thousands of years old.

The way the road across Balsam Gap and down Scotts Creek was described in the court orders. The court said to "lay out a road from David Weaver's at the head of Richland Creek to the Indian Bounty below the George Shuler place." Benjamin Odle was to be the overseer on part of the Scotts Creek Road from the ford of the first branch below James Bryson Jr.'s old place to the mill stone quarry, then three miles to the West side of David Wilson's to the Scotts Creek Road. John Stiles was to oversee the road down Scotts Creek from David Wilkins to the Indian Boundary. Another overseer, William Black, was to be responsible for the road from the stone quarry to the Indian Boundary below Jacob Shook's land. Among those mentioned in the road order was George Shuler, a German, who signed his name in German, Gorg Silzs. He and his wife, Mary, had six children—George, John, Jacob, David, Amanuel and Mary. He made his will June 12, 1803, but lived until 1826. He lived near the Indian Boundary.

The head of Richland Creek is above the Sara Ridge Road and the Mountain Spring Road above the Balsam Meadows division, close to the Balsam Gap on the south side. A road was made from the school branch below Robert Love's near Huley's cabin to the mill stone quarry on Scotts Creek. All who were living on the forks of Scotts Creek were to work on the roads. Consequently, the next part of the Scotts Creek Road is from the stone mill quarry to the public square in Waynesville. George Mingus was the overseer for this road at one time. Later, William Cathey Jr. was in charge of the repairs on the road from Waynesville to the mill stone quarry. In another road repair in 1812, John Eaton would be the one to oversee the maintenance on this road. The people on the David Cowell, Henry Smith Jr. and Thomas Love plantations were to do the work on this road.

The Waynesville Township High School at its second location, 1940. *Courtesy of Janet Webb.*

The building that housed the Central Elementary and is now used for private apartments. This was the location of the first Waynesville High School, 1989. *Courtesy of Janet Webb.*

All the road building was justified by the number of people who lived all along the way from Waynesville to the Indian Boundary. The first people registered deeds on the waters of Scotts Creek in 1806. They bought the land from others that had lived there before 1806. On April 12, Jacob Mingus sold land to Amos Brown. Then on September 26, George Cunningham sold one hundred acres for $100 to Elijah Johnson. Joseph Dobson was a neighbor, living near the large canebrake on the west side.

For more than a century, stories have been written and told that Abram M. Enloe was the birth father of Abraham Lincoln by his servant girl, Sarah. Enloe was supposed to have lived in Haywood County at this time. Although Enloe bought some land on Scotts Creek for five pounds on June 4, 1807, he continued to be a resident of Rutherford County, North Carolina. Enloe sold the land on both sides of Scotts Creek and a canebrake to James Brison for five hundred dollars on July 15, 1809. Enloe did not move to Haywood County until about 1820 and died before 1850. His wife's name was Sarah. This is the only Abram Enloe in the deeds. These stories have ignored the other members of Lincoln's family (he had an older sister) and ignored dates as well. Thus, it is very unlikely that Enloe had any connection with Abraham Lincoln.

In the following year, William McConnel paid $200 for some property on January 2. Also, he bought one hundred acres for $140 on May 20 on both sides of Patterson Fork, above the John Stiles home. Amos Brown also bought land on January 15. Li If H. Crow, a Cherokee, was a witness to this deed. George Gunter bought one hundred acres from John Fergus for $100 on April 2, 1808. This land was located on both sides of Judiculley Fork of Scotts Creek. Finally, George Cunningham Senior sold some land on a small tributary of Scotts Creek to George Cunningham Jr. for $84.50 on October 8. John Fergus was a witness on this deed. George Cunningham later sold one hundred acres for $400 to Humphrey Cunningham on March 16, 1810.

Several more people moved on to Scotts Creek in 1809. October 5, Thomas Jones obtained a State land grant and the next day, October 6, Joseph Dobson bought 320 acres on the left fork of Scotts Creek. In December, George Cunningham bought one hundred acres on the south side of the creek, crossing the dam and up both sides of the creek.

Others began to move into or buy land in the area over the next few years. They are Hugh Neely, John Morrow, James Wheeler, Solomon Messer, Elijah Johnson, George Hughes, Henry Wood, Alexander Coldwell and John Battle. One other, David Adams, bought one hundred acres for $38.87 at an auction in 1812. William Casheast, a Cherokee, had not paid the 1809 taxes. As a result, the Indian claim on this land had been lost.

After leaving the Scotts Creek area, the Tuckaseegee River is the next location continuing toward the town of Whittier. It was in this place that Richard Morrow sold land to Elijah Chastain on the Caney Fork of the Tuckaseegee River on August 15, 1809. This is near the location of the Judaculla Rock. Richard Morrow sold 144 acres for $500 to Benjamin Chastain on March 6, 1807. This

Main Street, Waynesville, when the street was red clay, 1900. *Courtesy of the* Enterprise Mountaineer.

Main Street before 1900. *Courtesy of the* Enterprise Mountaineer.

land was on both sides of Caney Fork of the Tuckaseegee River. January 29, 1810, Richard Morrow received $250 from Samuel Denton for some land on Caney Fork of the Tuckaseegee River.

Oconaluftee River, Soco Gap and Nearby Locations

When the county was formed, this area was the western end of the county. Today the Haywood–Jackson County line is on Soco Gap on U.S. 19A–441. On the south side of this highway is Hard Ridge. This is opposite the exit going down Jonathan Creek. Beyond Hard Ridge to the west are North Eagle Nest Mountain and Setzer Mountain, separated by Johnson Gap. On the north side of the road beyond Dellwood are Henry Knob, Killian Knob, Buck Mountain and Sheep Back Mountain. Maggie Valley is a large part of the settlement on this route between Dellwood and Soco Gap. In the Cherokee language, Soco was called "Ahalu Na," which means ambush. The Cherokee and the Shawnee Indians were enemies. The story was that the Cherokee won a battle with the Shawnee Indians in this place.

Walker Bald is a large mountain that is on the shoulder of the Cataloochee Divide. There are many names of locations that suggest people or activities that took place in the giving of these place names. Some of the names are Leatherwood Top and Middle Top on Walker Bald. Looking west are Potato Patch, Moody Top, Fie Top, Ned's Lick Gap, Pine Tree Gap and Little Bald Knob. Big Spring Cove's head is between the summit of Walker Bald and Leatherwood Top. Big Spring Branch flows out of this cove and goes through the middle of the Maggie Golf Course Country Club. Another open valley is back of the Olivet Church, watered by Evans Branch. West of Johnson Gap is a second open valley, watered by Johnson Branch, which joins Campbell Creek. As the highway starts up the mountain toward Soco Gap are Fie Creek and Carpenter Branch. These are in the area of "the most photographed scene in the Smokies," according to the sign beside a mounted viewing machine. These steep mountains and deep, narrow valleys are extremely popular with professional and amateur photographers alike.

At the beginning, a road would have to go over Soco Gap. It led to the rock barn to Robert Reed's on the Oconaluftee River. Another road went from the upper crossing of Soco at the rock camp to Robert Reece's property on the Oconaluftee River. A road started from the top of the mountain (Walker Bald) between head of Soco and Jonathan Creek and descended to the Indian Boundary and up the Oconaluftee River to Robert Roads place. A road was built between Robert Reed's house to the line of the property of John Hide on the Oconaluftee River. Another road was made from the ford of Oconaluftee River between John Hide's and Robert Reed's, turning into the new road that was cut out on the side of the river. William Welch was the overseer of the maintenance of the road from Robert Reed's for ten miles toward the gap

This is a view of the early 1900s North Main Street of Waynesville. This is after the paving of the street in 1904 and the common use of electricity, but before horse and wagon use ceased. *Courtesy of the* Enterprise Mountaineer.

Main Street just after it was paved. *Courtesy of the* Enterprise Mountaineer.

of the mountain between Jonathan Creek and Soco Gap, which included the workers on Oconaluftee River from Sam Edwards's property and up the river. Then John Parks became an overseer for the road, beginning at the gap of the mountain between the head of Jonathan Creek and Soco. In another order, Parks was commissioned to oversee the road as it traveled down Soco Creek until it intersected William Welch's property at the ten-mile post from Robert Reed's place. The road from Waynesville to the Indian Boundary was to be made a full fifteen feet, so that a wagon could travel this road. This order was made in March 1812.

Felix Walker had a grant for six hundred acres on Soco Creek on October 7, 1800. John Henry paid Felix Walker $200 for some land that was on both sides of Soco Creek. This was next to the John Dobson land. David McFarland and Eli Newman Henry were witnesses to this deed on January 5, 1807. On January 26, 1811, John Henry sold to John Dobson some land that he had bought from Felix Walker on Soco Creek. Second, in the year of 1804, others moved into the area. James Bird had a grant for 320 acres on Soco Creek on October 9, 1804. William Cathey bought 100 acres on the Oconaluftee River on December 10, 1804.

A little later in time, Jesse Cornwell sold some land to John Pick that lay on both sides of the Oconaluftee River. John Pick paid one hundred dollars on October 30, 1808. The next day, October 31, 1808, Benjamin Parks sold land, including a place called the Plumb Orchard on Ravens Ford to Jesse McFarland above the Jacob Mingus place for ninety dollars. Felix Walker was a witness to this deed. John Hyde had a grant on Shoal Creek for 50 acres. It was bounded by the Indian lands and Felix Walker's place. This was on October 21, 1809. John Hyde bought 200 acres on Raven Fork of the Oconaluftee River on December 25, 1809. Jesse Cornwell bought 250 acres on the North Fork of the Oconaluftee River in April 1811, and he in turn sold 150 acres to John Hyde on the same date.

One final resident of this area was Jacob Mingus, who bought land on both sides of the Oconaluftee River on a long bottom known as Big Cove. This was on September 23, 1812. On this same day, Jacob Mingus sold two hundred acres to Robert Love on Ravens Fork of the Oconaluftee River in Big Cove.

North of Waynesville

The Mystery of the Burnt Cabin and Mount Prospect

In 1913, the story started that Mount Prospect was the original name of Waynesville, a little village on this ridge, but Robert Love prevailed upon the people to change the name to Waynesville. However, this assumption is false.

There were no villages, only farms in Haywood County in 1808, except for some Indian villages in the western part of the county. In some things written about Haywood County it has been said that there were settlements in some of the areas of the farms. In the dictionary, a settlement is a few families living next to each other. As far as the deeds indicate, the property was for farms, not the small lots or pieces of land as found in a settlement. Later a settlement may have developed in some areas. Second, the court records state in several places that a road was to be built from the public square to Mount Prospect. There were only four ways to leave the public square—North Main Street, South Main Street, East Cross Street and West Cross Street. Third, after that first meeting at Mount Prospect, the court met in other private homes until the courthouse was built. If Mount Prospect had been near the mouth of Richland Creek, it would have been near the home of John Howell, where the June meeting was held. Did Mount Prospect prove to be inadequate after the March 1809 court meeting and the next stated time in June for the court to meet? Or could it have been that the travel ways were in disrepair? Fourth, in the June 1811 court session, the burnt cabin is said to be otherwise Mount Prospect. When did Mount Prospect burn? The only documented authorities concerning these two places are found in the minutes of the General Assembly of North Carolina and in the court minutes of the Haywood Court.

These records are located in the laws of North Carolina in 1808, part IV; First Book of Records of the Court of Pleas and Quarter Session of Haywood County, North Carolina. Next is the second part of the minutes starting with the

Looking east from the hill across Waynesville to Lickstone Ridge, early 1900s. *Courtesy of Janet Webb.*

In the early 1900s, Little Mountain between Plott Balsam and Eagles Nest Mountain (Mount Junaluska) on the west side of Waynesville. *Courtesy of Janet Webb.*

March Session in 1812. Also, there is the deed that Robert Love wrote in 1809 for more than seventeen acres. This was part of his farm.

Beginning in March 1809, the first court session to be at Mount Prospect was ordered by the General Assembly. The road orders for building roads and wagon roads usually stated that "they be laid out the best and easiest way." This meant to go through the valleys, as many of the mountains in Haywood County are steep. Looking at a raised map, it is easy to see the natural ways that people would travel. Then there was the precedent of the animal and Indian paths; these also went the easiest way.

The second reference was a road order from the burnt cabin up Jonathan Creek and across the mountain to the Rock Camp at Soco Gap. Men who worked on this road were James McFarland and all hands living on Jonathan Creek and those living on the Welch land. (Today, there is a fairly straight road going up the middle of Jonathan Creek valley from the Cove Creek and Interstate 40 intersection.) Jonathan Creek is several miles away from Waynesville. Soco Gap is west of Waynesville toward Cherokee. This route would go from Jonathan Creek through Maggie Valley and up the mountain to Soco Gap. Mount Junaluska is between this route and Waynesville.

There was also a road order from the east fork of Raccoon Creek road to the burnt cabin. Those men were the ones who had worked under John Tate as before. The Raccoon Creek road intersects with North Carolina Highway 209 South at the forks of the branches of east and west forks of Raccoon Creek where it becomes Raccoon Creek. The east fork of Raccoon Creek drains the land where the orchards of the Inmans and Franklins are, plus where the old grist mill still stands. How long was the road from Raccoon Creek to the burnt cabin?

In another reference to Mount Prospect, a wagon road order from the Town Square was given near Mount Prospect. The following men had been assigned to this road: Thomas Welch, James Welch, John Welch Senior and John Welch Jr., Lewis Smith, John Wikle and Thomas Love. Also, this order included Philip T. Burford, Edward Hyatt, Martin Buff, Mark Coleman, Jesse Tolers, Jonathan Osborn (who had a home in Flowery Gardens), John Howell and John Bellah. These men lived on the route and worked on the road. The town square was in Waynesville, but the Mount Prospect wagon road was in the country.

The next reference was for a road order from the public square to Mount Prospect. The men that were assigned to this project were the Welchs, Thomas Love, Gideon and Nathan Alman, Burford, Abraham Shook, David Nelson, David Powell, John Bryson, Henry Plott, Mark Coleman, Isaac Land, Howell, Hyatt and Elihu Chambers. Once again, there was an order to go from the center of town to Mount Prospect.

There were orders for a wagon road from Alexander's Ford (on Pigeon River, near the Warpath Ford) to the burnt cabin, otherwise Mount Prospect. The men who were to be on this project were those who lived on the route of the road. The names started with Elihu Chambers, Nicholas Ferguson, William Chastine, John McClure, George Cathey Jr. and Andrew McClure Sr. The next names

Louisa Methodist Church that was built on the camp meeting grounds on the Jacob Shook property, 2006. *Courtesy of Janet Webb*

were Jacob McFarland, Samuel McMullins, James Chambers, John Howell, Edward Hyatt and James Moore. The final group of names was Felix Walker, Ruben McFarland, Joseph McClure, James McClure, John Welch Senior, Hezehkiah Ellison, James Lovingood, and John McFarland, Esquire. Several of these men lived in the area of Chambers Mountain. This order refers to the burnt cabin as "otherwise Mount Prospect."

There remained four court orders of the roads to and from the burnt cabin location. The first order was to go from the burnt cabin to the Town of Waynesville. The men who were responsible for this road were Holliman Battle, Thomas Love, David Smith, Elihu Chambers, Abraham Eaton, William Chambers, John Ford, Jacob McFarland, George Cathey Jr., Archibald McHenry, Jonathan Osborn, James Stephenson, John Stephenson, John McDowell, Mark Coleman Jr., Daniel Fleming and Edward Hyatt. This was a road of some distance from Waynesville to the burnt cabin.

This old mill was built by William and his son, M.P. Francis, now located on Highway 276 south in Francis Cove, 1887. *Courtesy of the* Enterprise Mountaineer.

The old post office at Lake Junaluska. Mrs. R.C. Long was postmaster in the 1920s. *Courtesy of the* Enterprise Mountaineer.

The second order was to make John Howell the overseer to open a wagon road from the ford on Richland Creek below the buffs to the forks of the branch above the Howell's house. Next this wagon road was to intersect the road to be laid out from the burnt cabin to Waynesville. All hands who are able to work, living on the West side of Pigeon River from Jesse Owens near the bluffs of Richland Creek and including such hands as on Howell's plantation and those who work for Jonathan Osborn, were to do this job. This is more than five miles away from Waynesville, so the burnt cabin must have been around five miles from Waynesville.

Another order for a wagon road was placed from where John Welch Jr. now lives at the Thomas Welch's former plantation to the main road at the "burnt cabin (alias) Mount Prospect." The men responsible for this road were Thomas

Love, Holliman Battle, Andrew Welch, John Welch, Mark Coleman, William Coleman, David Nelson, Gideon Alman, Elihu McDowell, Lewis Smith, John Wikle, John Dillard, John Hood, William Allen, Edward Hyatt, James Welch, James Campbell and George Coleman. The statement 'burnt cabin (alias) Mount Prospect' is another bit of evidence that they were the same.

Additionally, the order was given for John Welch to be the overseer of the road from Waynesville to the top of the ridge above where he then lived, and along the way as he has already worked on toward the burnt cabin.

As to the question of the relationship between the burnt cabin and Mount Prospect, the records seem to support the idea that they may be the same. When did Mount Prospect burn? The first burnt cabin references are not connected to Mount Prospect by name, but in the September 1811 court minutes, the reference is made to the burnt cabin. The court met at Mount Prospect in March 1809, but not thereafter. Mount Prospect appeared to have burned before September 1811. The road orders list the burnt cabin or Mount Prospect as one of the locations for the road direction, direct to the north, even as far north, perhaps, as Cove Creek at the end of Jonathan Valley. Or could it have been where Richland Creek emptied into the Pigeon River, near the lands of Thomas Love and John Howell? Where was the real location of Mount Prospect? This is a two hundred-year-old mystery. The men who worked on these roads lived on the roads for which they were responsible. This was a clue as well as the directions from the public square to Mount Prospect. Who was the owner of this place called Mount Prospect? And what influence did he have in Raleigh when the laws were being made for the new county and its legal system? Could this have been Thomas Love?

I believe that after reading these records that Mount Prospect was a private home and it burned at some unknown date. I also believe that Waynesville was the only name of the county seat of Haywood County. From the time the deed was finished by Robert Love in November 1809 until January 1810, there was no other recorded name but Waynesville. Even though it became a village, the first thirteen lots were not sold until 1811 to John Welch. After this others began to buy lots and build.

The People of Jonathan Creek and North

Jonathan Valley is over five miles long and at places a little more than a mile wide. Jonathan Creek starts in Maggie Valley, turns north at Dellwood, then becomes the main creek in Jonathan Valley. The mouth of Jonathan Creek is on the Pigeon River just beyond Cove Creek. Other tributaries of Jonathan Creek in Jonathan Valley are Hemphill Creek between Walker Bald and Purchase Knob, Beantown Creek, Nelson Branch, Garrett Creek and Parks Branch. Germany Cove has a creek that flows into Hemphill Creek. On the slopes of the Cataloochee Divide to the West of Jonathan Valley are the mountains and coves where many of the people lived. These are the place names of the land, Henry

The old Cataloochee School had to close after the National Park System adopted Cataloochee, 1930s. *Courtesy of the* Enterprise Mountaineer.

Knob, Trit Knob, Walker Bald and Purchase Knob. Beyond the Cataloochee Divide to the northwest are the Cataloochee and Little Cataloochee Valleys. This area has been taken into the National Park. On the east of the valley are Utah Mountain and Goatrock Ridge. Coleman Gap is toward the northeast end of the valley, where the road was built to go to Iron Duff.

In March 1809, an order was given to build a road from the burnt cabin up Jonathan Creek, then across the mountain to the Rock Camp at the first crossing of Scotts Creek. However, this instruction is a bit questionable. The Plott Balsam Mountain is between Dellwood and Scotts Creek. Were they intending to build a road across this 4,500 feet high gap or go around the base of the mountain by way of Richland Creek Valley and Waynesville to Scotts Creek?

In the early years the county was divided into military companies. This designation was for military service of the home guard, voting places and for work orders of the court. Toward the end of the century military companies were changed to voting precincts and townships.

An order to make a new road was to be overseen by Hezekiah Ellison. This was starting from the forks of the road (between James McKee's and John Moody's) on Jonathan Creek to the lower field on Cove Creek and was to include the workers in Captain Henry's company below the house in which James Hemphill lived. Later, there was a road at the store above Shadrack Hyatt's place. This was the starting place of the new road to go to the right through a low gap to head up Jonathan Creek and to go to the stone house. Later a road was needed to go from the store up Jonathan Creek. William Shook was to assist. After starting from the forks of the road at McKee's and Moody's, the work was to end at the turnpike on Cove Creek. Captain Henry's company was to supply the workers of those who live below the house in which James Burford had lived. This was in the fall of 1812.

An order was made for Nicholas Ferguson to oversee roadwork from the forks of the road below the burnt schoolhouse on upper Jonathan Creek to the top of Balsam Mountain, which divides the waters of Soco and Jonathan Creeks. The workers designated lived above the former home of James Hemphill. James McKee was to oversee the roadwork beginning from the forks of the road below the burnt schoolhouse to the top of the mountain at the dividing of the waters between Soco Creek and Jonathan Creek. This roadwork started above Hemphill Creek and went to Soco Gap. In September 1812, there was a need for work on the road from the head of the creek on Balsam Mountain down to the ford above Malcolm Henry's home. John Leatherwood, who lived at the lower end of this work, was to oversee it, with those living on properties above his providing the workforce.

As time went on, wagon roads were also needed. During the year of 1810, a wagon road was to be built from Jonathan Creek—near where Thomas Coldwell had lived—to connect to another wagon road that went from the Pigeon River to Richland Creek. The way was through the gap of the mountain passing near the house where Isham Shook previously lived.

More road orders involved the construction of the turnpikes. The lower end of Jonathan's Creek exits into Cove Creek. This was the road connection to the turnpike, which had been on Cove Creek. In December 1812, John Moody was to oversee the work on the turnpike from Cove Creek to Big Creek. Hezekiah Ellison, a commissioner, was to visit the route that goes over Cataloochee Mountain (Cataloochee Divide) into Cataloochee Valley to make sure that it was in good order. When Hezekiah Ellison resigned his commission because he did not have the time needed to do the work, John Moody took his place. Moody was to attend to the business of making sure that the turnpike through Cataloochee Mountain, owned by Hugh and Mitchell Davidson, Esquires, stayed in good order. Moody made a report on the reasonable order of this turnpike.

Among the first people to settle in the valley of Jonathan Creek were John and Charles McDowell, who owned three hundred acres and may have been in the valley in 1790. Their neighbor, Thomas Hemphill, bought 940 acres from the State of North Carolina on the west fork of Jonathan Creek (Hemphill Creek), bordering the south line of the McDowells's property. Thomas Hemphill and James McDowell also bought six hundred acres and a good mill seat. All of the 1,540 acres were bought on January 4, 1792. Hemphill Creek flows from the Cataloochee Divide down the mountain between Walker Bald and Purchase Knob. Hugh Davidson had North Carolina State Grant No. 515, dated December 5, 1798, for a tract of land on Jonathan's Creek. He sold this tract to Robert Love on July 30, 1811.

Palmer Chapel at Cataloochee, 1990. *Courtesy of the* Enterprise Mountaineer.

On the same day, Robert Love sold some land that he owned to Hugh Davidson that was next to the Davidson land for the same price of the previous sale. This was a land exchange. Because the land value did not change, money may not have changed hands except on paper. Daniel McDowell had a North Carolina State Grant No. 23 for 200 acres near the Hezekiah Ellison place. This was entered on September 26, 1809. James McDowell died in early 1810, and the inventory to his estate was presented to the court in the March session of 1810. David McFarland was the administrator for his estate.

More transactions on Jonathan Creek included land sold between father and son, including negotiations involving William Davidson, who sold three hundred acres to his son, William Mitchell Davidson, on December 3, 1808. One of the boundary lines of this property crossed the Warpath and Jonathan Creek. On October 4, 1810, William Mitchell Davidson sold to his father, William Davidson, a part of the three hundred acres on the mouth of Jonathan Creek that crossed the Warpath. William Davidson bought one hundred acres that Benjamin Hide had previously purchased on March 1, 1808. This land was located below Cove Creek at the mouth of Jonathan's Creek and on the Pigeon River. Lastly, John Leatherwood acquired fifty-four acres on October 19, 1810. This land was on the wagon road on Jonathan Creek.

The son of John Walker, Felix Walker, was born in Virginia on July 19, 1753. John Walker brought his family to North Carolina. In about 1774, Felix traveled with Daniel Boone from North Carolina to Kentucky, where he was wounded and was forced to return home. Felix moved to Jonathan Creek. His North Carolina State Grant No. 996, October 7, 1800, was for two hundred acres on Jonathan Creek, the west side of the Pigeon River, including the place where John Hide bought land. Next to his own land and that of James McKee's, Walker bought another fifty acres on October 6, 1809. Then he bought another one hundred acres on December 14, 1811. As a merchant, Walker had stores in Waynesville, Scotts Creek and Quallatown. He bought and sold land and was a soldier, farmer, merchant and lawyer. Walker also served in Congress from 1817 through 1821. Felix Walker coined the term "buncombe," meaning to continue in long debate or speech, when he filibustered the sixteenth Congress when talking about Buncombe County. Walker made a will in November 13, 1826, as he was about to make a trip to Mississippi. He left his estate to his son, Joseph H. Walker, and died in Mississippi in 1828.

Milas Messer was born in 1865 and died in 1963. His life on Cove Creek was an example of the way that folks lived in the rural areas. He was a farmer, kept bees for honey, had an apple orchard, raised cane for his molasses and was a blacksmith! He was a gunsmith as well. But Messer's talents did not stop with these abilities. He tanned his own leather and made the neighbors shoes. He also made coffins. including lots of beautiful baby coffins.

There was not much opportunity for education in Cove Creek, but Milas Messer learned to read. He took an hour at lunch every day to rest, eat and read his Bible before returning to work. His wife, Nancy, was busy with her duties. She did her wash with a washboard in a special place near the creek. She had an iron kettle in which to heat water for the wash. She dried fruit on a rock near the creek. Other chores included housework, cooking meals, clothes to make and her large flower garden that she tended. In addition to this, she and Milas raised thirteen children.

In the last valley across the Cataloochee Divide from Jonathan Creek, the first land entry of 1814 was made in Cataloochee by Thomas Coldwell. He had one hundred acres. Born in 1792 to Henry Coldwell, originally of Pennsylvania, Coldwell used his land to build a cabin in which to stay while caring for the animals that roamed free, a popular practice at the time. His brother, William, born 1787, bought land and lived in Cataloochee. The other brother, James, born 1795, was the father of Levi Coldwell. (There was another Coldwell, named William Coldwell Sr. (1755–1837), who lived there, but may not have been any kin to the first family.) The other people to live in the great valley were the families of Palmer, Noland, Bennett, Hannah and others. Men from Jonathan Creek came into the valley to hunt and run cattle. These men would have claims on night cabins in the area. It wasn't until the mid-1830s that the first people became permanent settlers in the Cataloochee Valley. Then others moved into Little Cataloochee by the early 1850s. For one hundred years a lot of folks were born, lived, went to school, to church and were buried in these two valleys. Even some terrible events took place in the Civil War in this remote valley. But the National Park Service decided to make a park in the early 1930s and by 1937 nearly all the families had moved away. Only a few houses, two church buildings, a few out buildings, some barns and a school building remain.

CRABTREE AND IRON DUFF

Bald Creek and Liner Creek form the headwaters of Crabtree Creek. These two creeks join near the foot of Lee Mountain in the Upper Crabtree section. Crabtree Creek runs between Messer Mountain and Mill Mountain to empty into the Pigeon River a couple of miles beyond these two mountains. There are several fair sized coves on either side of the creek. Rush Fork is a large tributary of Crabtree Creek.

In this beautiful, wild and remote land it was necessary for people to travel. Therefore a road order was made in 1809 to find the nearest, best and most convenient way to Buncombe County. There was a trail from Crabtree over Newfound Mountain into Sandy Mush in Buncombe County. (It would seem to us today with the roads that we have that the natural course of the road would have been to travel from Crabtree to Lake Junaluska to Clyde then east to Buncombe County. But at that time this may have been thought as a roundabout way because of the other roads that were in existence in the county.) The Baptist Church was organized in Crabtree in the very early 1800s, sponsored by Newfound Baptist Church in Leicester, Buncombe County. It was from the Crabtree road near the Crabtree (Baptist) meeting house to the house of Robert Phillips, Esquire, which a new road was to be laid out in 1809. David

Scroggs was to oversee the road from the forks of Crabtree Creek (below the old Crabtree/Iron Duff school) to the upper end of the mountain below Jacob Shook's (Clyde) on the road leading to Hominy Creek. This may have become North Carolina 209 South, which followed Hyder Mountain Road to Clyde before heading east to Hominy.

Another church that was built in Crabtree was the Mount Zion Methodist Church. It was first built of logs in 1850. Many years later in 1882,when this log structure burned, it was replaced with a brick building. This was the first brick church to be erected in Haywood County. It is also the oldest church building in the county.

The next road to be made was from the Crabtree road near the Crabtree mill to Fines Creek, where an Indian Trail crosses the creek. This may have been the road to start at the junction of Crabtree Road and Rush Fork Road before going down the Riverside Road to Rabbit Skin Road to Fines Creek. Another road was on Rush Fork, the north side of Crabtree Creek and then down to the Pigeon River. Finally the road went down the southwest side of the river to the mountain next to Jonathan Creek (the backside of Utah Mountain) and up as high as the dividing ridge above the Widow Shook Branch. The workers were members of Captain Thompson's company. This appears to be part of North Carolina Highway 209 and the Riverside Road.

Another, Archibald McHenry, was to oversee the Crabtree road, beginning at the first branch below James Thompson's plantation and going to the rocky branch above Davidson's, as surveyed by the road jury. Those workers were on Crabtree down to McHenry's mill in Captain Henderson's company and helped build the road through Stephenson's plantation before it intersected with the old road at the mill. On the north side of the Pigeon River all the way to Osborn's, workers constructed roads from the dividing ridge at Widow Shook's branch, up the Pigeon River to the mouth of Richland Creek. A road was also needed from Fines Creek and Crabtree to an intersection at the road from Waynesville to Asheville, possibly near where Lake Junaluska was eventually constructed. Special attention was given to the road from the forks near the Crabtree Creek Mill to the ford on Givins Creek. A ford was needed and the road was to be fifteen feet wide on level ground and ten feet wide in the difficult places and short turns in the road, in order for a wagon to make any sharp turns. Finally, another wagon road was needed to go from the forks of the Crabtree road near James Stephenson to Waynesville.

Then there is a question concerning Peter Mason who settled on Crabtree Creek about 1800. No deed was recorded for him, so one wonders if he squatted on the land or rented it. He lived to be about 107 years old. Peter was one of the earliest people to live in this area. He was born in about 1785. Peter Mason married Caroline McClure and their children were Caroline, Elizabeth, John, Mariah, Nancy Adeline, James M. and Peter William. He died about 1892. Deeds regarding land in Crabtree began to be recorded in 1804. On August 3 of that year, David McDowell purchased one hundred acres from Nathan Deaver for $100. This land was on both sides of Crabtree Creek and was the end tract of land originally granted to John McDowell. Samuel M. Mullen and Robert Reed were witness to this transaction. Next on November 7, 1804, John Strother sold William James eighty-seven acres for $25 on the brush fork of Crabtree Creek. His neighbors were Ross and McDowell. He had George Strother and James Bryson to witness his deed.

In a second group of sales, David Scruggs bought two hundred acres on Crabtree Creek for $435. These acres were the same three different tracts granted to different people previous to Scruggs's ownership: twenty-two acres to Hugh Davidson, fifty-seven acres to Henry and Ragsdale and the rest to David Allison. This land went through the hands of the Sheriff of Buncombe County to John Strother. It was then sold to William McConnel, who sold it to David Scruggs on January 13, 1807. John Stevenson and Archibald McHenry were witnesses for this deed. The deed chain was recorded in the deed, which gave these details.

On the North Fork of Crabtree Creek, on June 17, 1809, Colley Jackson paid $80 for 100 acres. This acreage was next to the Ragsdale 100-acre survey. Then on August 4, 1810, Colley Jackson sold to Andrew McClure these 100 acres for $230. Next to Jackson's land on the north fork of Crabtree Creek, George Crawford bought 100 acres for $130 on December 26, 1809. Thomas McClure bought some additional land next to the land on which he lived. Andrew McClure sold to Thomas McClure 13 acres of his land for $60, with James Al Ellis signing as a witness on March 20, 1810. Thomas C. St. Clair paid $284 to John Strother through Robert Love, his attorney, for the 568 acres of land next to George Crawford on December 21, 1811. On this same day, St. Clair bough 900 more acres for $400 on Sandy Mush Creek, which is on the shoulder of Sandy Mush Bald (on the Haywood County line). This property was next to George Crawford and Captain James Lowness's land in Silvers Cove.

John Wilkins bought 140 acres on both sides of Rush Fork Creek. John Wilkins paid George Lovil £100. On March 3, 1810, George Lovil was still living on the property, which was above Samuel Rogers's land, when he sold it. There were two men, who were both named John Woody. They signed as witnesses. This property is located on the present-day North Carolina 209.

Robert Ferguson and his wife, Frances Love Ferguson, had eight children. Their home was on Rush Fork at the base of Cedar Cliff Mountain. In honor of the Ferguson family, the name of Cedar Cliff Mountain was changed to Ferguson Mountain, which was recognized in Raleigh in 1977. There was a ceremony at the Crabtree Baptist Church for this memorial naming of the mountain.

Joseph McCracken and his family lived in Upper Crabtree. They moved there in 1811. Joseph married Sarah Vaughn in 1798. The McCrackens had thirteen children. He lived his entire life in North Carolina, from 1776 to 1848. Joseph is buried in the Crabtree Cemetery.

Aaron McDuff, a Scotsman, settled on his land a little before 1820. His neighbors began to call him Duff. Then in 1873 when a post office was located in the community, the government gave it the name Iron Duff. It was not always so easy to go from Iron Duff to Crabtree. There was the Pigeon River to cross.

So before a bridge was constructed, the best way was to use a boat. There was a dairy farm in Iron Duff. The truck that picked up to milk to take it to the store was on the Crabtree side of the river. That meant that the dairyman had to made boat trips across the Pigeon River both ways, twice a day, seven days a week. He was not the only person to use this community boat, as there were about four other families in this part of Iron Duff. If one could not cross the river, then the people traveled up the Iron Duff road. This road was long and only used when the river was too high to cross in a boat.

Fines Creek, Twelve Mile Creek and Crystal Creek

The location of Fines Creek is a remote valley, surrounded by mountains with one natural outlet. Oak Knob is on the southeast side of the natural entrance of Fines Creek valley. To the east of the knob is Rush Fork Gap that separates the knob from Messer Mountain. This high mountain is topped by Rich Top and Sandymush Bald. The Haywood County and Madison County line follow the ridgeline of the Newfound Mountain to the northeast. Hurricane Mountain forms a wall to the north. The mouth of Fines Creek as it flows from the Fines Creek valley goes by Shelton Laurel before it empties into the Pigeon River at Hepco. The Hepco Dam was destroyed in 1966. This valley is very accessible today by North Carolina Highway 209, which crosses Rush Fork Gap from Crabtree into Fines Creek, but this ease of travel was not always the case. The land was good for growing crops in the small fields, and nice little meadows dappled this remote mountain basin. For the frontier man who liked the isolated life, this area was ideal. To this day, the area around Fines Creek remains a pristine land.

Peter Fines was one of the mountain boys who had fought under John Sevier at King's Mountain. Peter lived across the mountain in Tennessee when Indians stole some of his horses. Peter and others went after the horses, but Peter was slain in the process. His friends could not bury him as it was wintertime and the ground was frozen. They broke a hole in the ice to put his body there until they could bury it and marked the location by a blaze on a tree and a pile of rocks. When they returned, Peter's body was gone. The naming of Fines Creek was in honor of Peter Fines. (The weather is more severe in Fines Creek than in the Waynesville area, and there is a popular saying, "If in snows anywhere, it will snow here first.")

Some of the first people to purchase land in Fines Creek were buying land in the late 1700s. First was John McDowell Sr., who had some land that was surveyed on October 24, 1794. This land lay between the Pigeon River, Crystal Creek and Camp Creek. After his father's death, John McDowell Jr. sold about two hundred acres by a sheriff's sale to pay debts against the John McDowell Sr. estate on March 16, 1812. Other owners began purchasing Fines Creek Land around 1798, including the Revolutionary War veterans David Russell, Hugh Rogers and John Penland. Hugh Rogers was born in 1761 in Pennsylvania and fought under Robert Love in 1788. Hugh married Nancy Thornton on

October 28, 1789. He and Nancy had twelve children: David, born August 27, 1790; John H., born 1792; Andrew Newton, born 1793; James Bayles and Matthew Nathan, born February 4, 1798; Hugh, born July 12, 1801; Thornton Fontaine and Robert, born February 24, 1805; Cyrus, born July 10, 1807; Jesse William, Barnard and Nicholas Powers, born in 1813. This next man, Robert Rogers, names his wife, Joane, in his will, which was probated in 1822. Was Rogers kin to the Hugh Rogers who fought in the American Revolutionary War? Likewise William Parham names his wife, Peggy, as well as a son, William, and daughter-in-law, Catherine. This will was probated in 1824. Was the Parham family connected to the Baptist Minister, Posey Parham?

The last to purchase land in Fines Creek in the eighteenth century, Robert Henry received North Carolina State Grant No. 754 for 250 acres that lay on both Crystal Creek and the Pigeon River on December 18, 1799. Henry died October 29, 1848, in Haywood County.

In the next century, on January 10, 1803, Joseph Dobson paid two hundred shillings for North Carolina State Grant No. 1730. Dobson's land was 400 acres on the west side of Pigeon River above Robert Reed's place, including property formerly owned by John Penland. The John Penland farm was on the mouth of Crystal Creek (Fines Creek) on the Pigeon River near Hepco at the base of Oak Knob. Five years later, on August 18, 1808, Robert Penland, the son of John, bought 320 acres on Crystal Creek for $800. John Wilson had owned this land. William Mehaffey and T. Howard were witnesses to this deed. It is said that Robert Penland was a Revolutionary soldier. This grant was on August 8, 1809, is for Joseph Maxwell who had North Carolina Grant No. 17 for 200 acres on a small creek of Fines Creek near the John Wilson's lower boundary line.

Finally, after these people had started living on Fines Creek, a wagon road had to be surveyed out from Fines Creek through the Pigeon settlement to the courthouse. This was to be the best and shortest way possible in 1810. A new road was needed going from the upper settlement of Fines Creek to intersect the road that goes from the courthouse in Waynesville and down Crabtree Creek in 1811. This road may be North Carolina 209 as we know it today. Although the records state that the road was to be made, later people had to use the river to get from Fines Creek to Crabtree for many years.

Levi Sutton, his wife, Sally McGaha, and three children, formed another family that lived in Fines Creek. The couple moved there soon after they were married. Levi was born in 1826 and died in 1863. He was killed in a raid at his home during the Civil War. Sally lived from 1830 until 1918. The children were Elizabeth (1849–1929), John (born 1851) and Jesse James (born 1858).

Another person of note was Daisy Cecil Brown. She was born in a log cabin on Hurricane Mountain on December 31, 1906. She joined the Salvation Army as a young woman. In 1934, Brown came back to the mountains to start many preaching stations and schools and a mission at Maple Springs. She traveled much of the time by horseback and provided badly needed help for the area. She was known and loved for many years. Later, she founded The

Citadel on Max Patch, the only rural Salvation Army post in the United States. Major Brown died in Fines Creek of cancer on December 4, 1958. Brown was buried in the Hurricane View Cemetery. She held the Salvation Army's highest award—the Order of the Founder—and the twenty-five-year medal for "faithful and honorable service."

South of Waynesville

Allens Creek

Allens Creek is an open valley to the south of Waynesville and contains the 8,030-acre watershed and reservoir for Waynesville. Roberson Ridge and Quinland surround this reservoir. The creek below the overflow of the dam is a clear, cold stream. There are plenty of river rocks, moss, bushes and trees that make this area a beautiful, calm place. A little further down the creek where a residential area begins is a modern rock quarry. As the stream goes down Balsam Mountain, Cove Field Ridge, Big Cove and Pinnacle Knob are on the west. On the east are Roberson Ridge and Marge Mountain. Medford Branch, Browning Branch, Rocky Branch and Cove Field Branch are some streams that flow into Allens Creek.

One of the early people to settle this section was William Allen, a Revolutionary War soldier, who purchased 640 acres in 1804. He may have been the one who gave the name to the community of Allens Creek. George Cunningham bought part of this section of land from William Allen and built a log house in about 1805. The Cunningham descendents are restoring the old log house that was the George Cunningham home. Others who were neighbors of William Allen were John and James Welch in 1808. Next, other property owners on Allens Creek were Adam Killian, Thomas St. Clair and William Bryan. Then, on April 13, 1807, Adam Watson paid twenty-five shillings for North Carolina State Grant No. 1632 for fifty acres that lay on a small creek south of Richland Creek, which joined the land of William Allen on the south side of Andrew Green Robinson's property. A path going to Adam Watson's home was constructed on the Robinson land. Watson paid $130 for 130 acres on March 23, 1805. This had been the John Hack place on Richland Creek. George Strother and Hugh Neeley were witness to this sale. Finally, William Allen bought a quit claim on 251 acres for $20, where William Cathey had formerly lived. This was a little more than one half-mile from the side of the mountain near a fork of Richland

Creek, which became Allens Creek. Samuel Hollingworth was a witness to this deed on June 5, 1809.

There is a community park and several churches on the road that starts at the intersection with South Main Street of Waynesville and continues up Allens Creek to the overflow of the reservoir.

HAZELWOOD

This little village was incorporated in 1905. The first two mayors of Hazelwood are W.W. Quinland and W.H. Cole. When Mr. Cole, who was born in Pennsylvania, came to Haywood County in 1893, he made his home in what became Hazelwood. At that time the land was a swampy area. Because of the high water table, the homes in Hazelwood did not have basements. After Mr. Cole started a sawmill, more people made their homes in the new village. Cole named the town Hazelwood.

Here are some other things of interest about Hazelwood. The town did not have electricity until the mid-1910s. Around 1920, the streets began to be paved. Roberta Snyder was the first postmaster in 1913. The first church services were all held in the same building, be they Baptist, Methodist or Presbyterian. Miles Parton was the blacksmith. The first police officer in Hazelwood was Thomas Singleton.

The first of two businesses in Hazelwood was the Junaluska Leather Company (referred to as the Tannery). The Tannery burned in 1993. And the second business was the Hazelwood Manufacturing Company. It went out of business when the production moved to other locations. One of the largest fires in Hazelwood was in 1982 when Benfield Industries burned. There were lots of chemicals involved. Hazelwood became a ghost town until the fire was out and

The old Hazelwood School, 1985. *Courtesy of the* Enterprise Mountaineer.

A store in Hazelwood near the train depot in the early history of Hazelwood, 1910.
Courtesy of the Enterprise Mountaineer.

The First Baptist Church in Hazelwood behind the old Hazelwood school, 1940s.
Courtesy of the Enterprise Mountaineer.

Framers Creek in Hazelwood with the old water tower in the background, 1990s. *Courtesy of the* Enterprise Mountaineer.

it was safe to return. Many years passed before the EPA said that it was safe to build on that property.

Other large businesses that have been in Hazelwood and are no longer there are the Rag Mill, a tapestry mill, and Dayco, which made parts for automobiles from rubber or plastic. One manufacturing business, which stayed, was the headquarters of Wellco-Research. They make military boots.

The Hazelwood Elementary School was built in 1923. A new modern school has been built in a new location. The old building was being used for several non-profit services. One of which was Folkmote, an international cultural festival. Folkmote is celebrated in July of each year.

Hazelwood was a town until 1995, when it merged with Waynesville. Hazelwood still has its own post office with boxes for its citizens. The Main Street of Hazelwood has been renamed Hazelwood Avenue.

Somewhere in Haywood County

The County at Large

The county was divided into military companies, and each one was to be assigned a justice of the peace. The following list is for 1809: Abraham Eaton was the justice of the peace for Captain John McFarland's Company (Cruso, east fork of the Pigeon River); William Deaver was the justice of the peace for Captain William Cathey's Company (Lake Logan, west fork of Pigeon River); Archibald McHenry was the justice of the peace (Crabtree) for Captain James Thomson's Company, which later became Captain Jacob McFarland's Company; Benjamin Odle was the justice of the peace (Scotts Creek) for Captain Thomas Dobson's Company; Holliman Battle, was the justice of the peace (Richland Creek) for Captain James Wheeler's Company; John Dobson was the justice of the peace for Captain Benjamin Dobson's Company; Hugh Davidson was the justice of the peace (Jonathan Creek) for Captain William McFarland's Company. The locations in the parentheses are the location of the homes of the justices or of the captains and may be the location of the military company. The Companies in 1811 (for tax purposes and the justices of the peace to take the lists of taxable property for the present year) were: David Russell stood for Captain James Stephenson Company; John McFarland stood for the McFarland Company; William Deaver stood for Captain Simmons Company; Thomas Love stood for Captain Robert Love's Company; John McCracken stood for Captain Chambers Company; Hugh Davidson stood for Captain Henry's Company; and John Dobson stood for the Lufty Company.

A county election was to be held in Waynesville in 1811. The persons to be the inspectors in the election were Benjamin Odell and George Cathey (east fork) for Beaverdam; Thomas McClure, Esquire, Benjamin Clark and George Hall for Scotts Creek; John McCracken, Esquire, Daniel Black and James Curthers for Oconaluftee; and John Dobson, Esquire, William Welch Sr. and

Benjamin Parks. The court did not record what county offices were to be filled or the date on which the election was to be held. The court order was in March.

Joseph Sisk was approved to build a public mill on his own land on the forks of Fines Creek in 1810. Holliman Battle wanted to have a business in his home in Waynesville, called an ordinary or a place of custom, also known as a tavern. It was granted. A year later Battle asked to have his license renewed. Robert Love, the court clerk, was paid fifty shillings for the two-year's work on the tax lists and the certificates that were issued.

James Welch became the attorney for Edward Hayes for the purpose of securing legal bounty land from Georgia. He did service as a soldier for two years and six months under General John Clark in Georgia. He wanted 640 acres of land. The date of this document is April 1, 1809. Edward was living in Haywood County in 1810. But he must have been able to get his bounty land, because this is the last time he is mentioned in the records. These types of records help the DAR to locate the graves of American Revolutionary War veterans.

The first tax money had been collected in the county. The first use of this money was for ten pounds to be given to Nathaniel Thompson for the benefit of the poor, specifically for taking care of a deranged woman named Betsy Goodwin. There is no further information on this woman: how long she lived or what relationship she was to Thompson. Nathaniel Thompson died between 1820 and 1830.

In 1811, William Davis Sr. was brought into court on charges of assault and battery and was fined ten dollars. The next day the fine was rescinded. In this court of 1809, an order was made for the children of Susannah and Ben Yount to be brought into court by the sheriff and to be dealt with as the law directs. Whether the children had done a criminal act or a criminal act was done to them is unclear.

A question as to the last will and testament of John Hughes was also addressed in court. Margaret and George Hughes said it was the last will and testament of John Hughes. And that they were to be the executors. James Hughes, one of the heirs, said that it was not the will of John Hughes. The court would have to decide. Unfortunately, the results of such court cases were not always published.

On the next day, the court ordered that Jacob Shook and John Fulbright were to be appointed administrators of the estate of John Shook, deceased. On that same day a court order was given to Daniel McDowell and William Stevens to sell the perishable property of John Morrision, deceased, and to make an account of his property in a timely manner. Following in March 1810, Daniel McDowell made an inventory of the estate of John Morrison

On Monday, December 25, 1809, Anna McDowell, widow of James McDowell, gave an affidavit that David McFarland should be the administrator of the estate of James McDowell. He was permitted to sell all private property of the McDowell estate and to give an accounting of the sale in the March term of court. Then the court appointed four of the esquires to cut the provision alloted by law to Anna McDowell. Thomas McClure was appointed guardian to Margaret and

James McDowell, minor orphan children in June 1811. It was on this date that the final settlement showed that $16 was for the work of the executor. The balance of the estate, $105.29, was put in the hands of Thomas McClure, the guardian of the children.

The court ordered Jacob Shook and John Fulbright to make an inventory of the estate of John Chambers. Phillip T. Burford was appointed guardian of Mary Chambers and John Chambers, the two older children of the six orphans of James Chambers. Burford had in his possession notes from George Cathey and Joseph Chambers for $115.09½, from James Walker for $2.02, from John Patton Jr. for $2.12, from James McKcc for $92.12 and from Joseph Chambers for $7.00. There was also listed: one feather bed, one bolster, two pillows, two sheets, two counterpanes, one glen pot and one bed quilt. Mary Chambers had not received money for work she had done. Finally, William Deaver was appointed guardian to Rachel, George, William David and James Chambers—four orphan children under the age of fourteen years of James Chambers. Deaver received $409.02 from the estate for the children's care.

The will of Samuel Hollingsworth was produced in court and proved by William Deaver. On Tuesday, December 25, 1810, George Cathey and James Cathey, of East Fork, were appointed administrators of the estate of Daniel Cathey. A committee of four was appointed to check the estate value of Daniel Cathey for the purpose of making an allotment for the widow, Jemima Cathey, and her children for the coming year. On September 1811, John Fergus and Thomas Love, executors of the estate of John Bevin, deceased, were paid for their work.

The next items are legal matters of dispute. In September 1809, an order was given for a process against William Evans for an unnamed problem. The next was a problem between neighbors. A new survey was needed for the disputed line between the properties of John Hide and Robert Reed on the Oconaluftee River. This dispute had occurred several times. It seems that neither Hide nor Reed were satisfied with any of the surveys done by other surveyors before Robert Love. Robert Love became the surveyor for this Hide and Reed boundary line after others had made several surveys. Perhaps they were finally satisfied. They never came to court again about this matter. Nuisance charges by the state were brought against Elihu Chambers and Andrew Welch. Both were found guilty in 1811. In the same court, assault and battery charges were brought against William Welch. He pled guilty and paid a fine of fifteen shillings. Then as now, people resorted to civil law suits to settle boundary line disputes, fights between men and quarrels between neighbors.

The first Court of Pleas and Quarter Session of Haywood County was held on Monday, March 27, 1809 at the location of Mount Prospect. A year later, March 1810, a road order was given to locate a route for a wagon road to be built from the public square to the wagon road near Mount Prospect, 'be done in the nearest and best way.' Then, June 1810, a court order was given to mark the route of this road from the public square to Mount Prospect. Later, in December 1812, a road order was given to survey a route for a wagon road from where John Welch Jr.

lived at Thomas Welch's former plantation to the main road at the burnt cabin (alias) Mount Prospect. The men responsible for this job were Thomas Love, Holliman Battle, Andrew Welch, John Welch, Mark Coman, William Coleman, David Nelson, Gideon Alman, Elihu McDowell, Lewis Smith, John Wikle, John Dillard, John Hood, William Allen, Edward Hyatt, James Welch, James Campbell and George Coleman. Lastly, in this same court, an order was given for John Welch to be an overseer of the road from Waynesville. He was to start at the top of the ridge above where he lived. Then Welch was to continue toward the burnt cabin. This was the route he had followed before.

A slave deed was made on September 16, 1811 for William Colvard, the son of John Colvard and Juda Merryman Colvard, of Haywood County for some slaves that were willed to him. His mother, Juda Colvard, had received these slaves from, her father, John Merryman of Cumberland County, Virginia. William's father was John Colvard of Surrey County, North Carolina. These slaves were named Peter and Ursula and any children they may have had. James Welch became the attorney for William Colvard to receive the slaves that were left to William in his mother's will. Later, Jesse Anderson sold two slaves, Nathan, and Sosey, his wife, to John Nelson. The slave couple was both about thirty-seven years old. Anderson received $750 for them in June 1812. Finally, in a deed of July 5, 1812, Thomas Dillard and Parkes Daris Dillard, his wife both of Washington County, Tennessee, left to their children: Artemesia Petit Dillard, John Love Dillard and Ester Dillard, three slaves. These three slave females were named Margaret, Disy and her child, Usly.

There were only a few families who had slaves in Haywood County, the Loves, Colvards, Osbornes, Welchs, Andersons, Nelsons and the Dillards. There may have been another family or two who had a few slaves. The slaves were prone to stay with a given family and there was not very much slave trading. There were a few deeds of gift slaves to a family member. The land was hilly and precluded the need for a slave. Slaves were expensive to buy and to maintain. Therefore, most families worked to make enough crops to survive with not much produce left to sell.

LAKE JUNALUSKA

Sometimes the Richland Creek Valley was called Tuscola. Before 1913, the Richland Creek Valley that eventually became Lake Junaluska contained farmland. The Ward farm, in the valley that was sold to the Methodist Church, was located below the cliffs that were part of the Asbury Trail. This trail became a walking path from the bridge over the dam to the George R. Stuart Auditorium. This large circular building was first an open pavilion. Then large windows were installed. The windows kept the birds out—as well as the weather—when a meeting was taking place. The J.T. Coman farm was located at the auditorium site. Richland Creek had flowed through this valley. The Methodist Church wanted to build a retreat and a meetingplace. Many of the people of the church wanted to build homes at the retreat as well, and a dam was built to form a lake. When the lake was lowered in the winter to remove silt, the path of the Richland Creek bed was revealed. The upper lake was shallower than the rest of the lake, and it contained lots of cattails and other marsh growth. In the late 1920s, young people would paddle a flat bottom boat at night and gig bullfrogs in this marsh. Eventually, a part of the upper lake was filled with soil and it was used as solid land for new buildings and a sports area. The marsh is now gone.

Hills, mountains and meadows surround Lake Junaluska. Starting at the bridge over the dam and turning north, the road climbs steeply to the peak where the lighted cross stands. Beyond the cross to the north was Susie Knob. It was on Susie Knob that the first thirteen homes were built after the lake was completed.

Some of the people who came there for that first summer had to carry water from a central water source and use candles for lighting. Among the family names of the first homes were George Stuart, John Pepper, C.E. Weatherby, J.A. Bullock, Bishop Atkins and James Cannon Jr. Crum Cottage, the home of Dr. Mason Crum was built in 1919. Another of these first homes was Come-Up-Lodge. It was built on a bank on Lake Shore Drive. It was removed to Cokesbury Circle in the late 1990s when the new headquarters building was being built. This building was designed to look like the Old Epworth Rectory in England, the home of the Wesley family. The Lambuth Inn, which was located on the same hill as the cross, was built in 1922. This was the same year that the cross was erected on the hill overlooking the lake. One of the first buildings for religious education was Shackford Hall, built in 1923, although the interior of this building was not completed until the mid-1950s.

On the gentle rolling hills surrounding the lake are many beautiful homes. Many years ago when there was a depot on the railway, wild strawberries could be picked in June in some of these meadows on South Lake Shore Drive. Homes have been built in those meadows.

A business, the Junaluska Supply, later known as the Liner building, provided building materials and other items needed in the home for over seventy years. Also, groceries were sold and a post office was included in the complex. After the business closed and the post office was relocated, the building was destroyed in a controlled burn in 1997 to make way for new condominiums.

A walking path was built that encircles a part of the lake. The walking path is about two and a half miles long. A long footbridge that is part of the walking path crosses the narrows where the waist of Lake Junaluska separates the lower and upper lakes.

Back in the early years of the lake, there was a large wild grapevine growing on a tree that overhung the narrows on the western deep side of the water. Some of the adventurous young people would use this vine to jump into the water. This was also before the days of the swimming pool and those who wanted to swim did so in the lake. They made rafts or used boats to navigate the lake. Then there were some good swimmers who would swim the mile in the lake from a point near the narrows to the dam. For several generations of people, this has been a place to create good memories.

More than fifty years ago at Lake Junaluska. The old wooden Cherokee boat dock is in the foreground, 1940s. *Courtesy of the* Enterprise Mountaineer.

The bridge over the dam at Lake Junaluska. Liner's store and the post office have been replaced by condominiums, 2006. *Courtesy of Janet Webb.*

Many have good memories of the old Cherokee Boat. People would ride it for pleasure as it circled the lake. It had a practical use as well. Until the late 1930s, people would come all over the southeastern United States and arrive at the lake by train. There were as many as four passenger trains a day going as well as freight trains. There was a boathouse on that side of the lake. The new arrivals and their baggage would be loaded on the boat and ferried across the lake to the homes and hotels. The train service was closed before 1966, when the depot was closed. Although the depot was moved away from the railway, the building was saved and became a private home within a mile of the original location.

There are lots of wild ducks, geese, coots, swans and other wild fowl that come to the lake, some to live for a season and some for the entire year. These wild birds are not frightened of people. The fowl want to be fed with shelled corn and bread scraps. When folks come close to the shore edge where the birds are, they will come quacking and honking, begging for a handout.

MAGGIE VALLEY

The Setzer cabin was one of the first cabins in the valley that became Maggie Valley. This cabin was part of the main house at Mountain Joy. The one-room cabin was a combination dining room and the business office. In 1904 Mr. John Sidney Setzer's daughter's name, Maggie, was chosen for the name of a post office. The post office was to be in a corner of Setzer's parlor. As a result the valley that surrounded this post office took the name Maggie. Maggie Setzer became a mascot for the area. There was a special costume—a red skirt, a green blouse and a yellow apron and poke bonnet—for the woman who played the part of Maggie in the summer. The real Maggie died in 1979. The town's name became official as Maggie Valley in 1974.

High mountains surround Maggie Valley. The slopes of Sheep Back Mountain, Buck Mountain, Walker Bald, Setzer Mountain and Eagle Nest Mountain are a part of the community called Maggie Valley. The homes are in this valley and on the slopes of the surrounding mountains and in the coves. The road that follows Jonathan Creek up the mountain started as an Indian trail before the court ordered to build a road from Dellwood through Maggie Valley to Soco Gap. This road over Soco Gap from the Cherokee lands was the way the Indians would travel to Waynesville and points east.

Campbell Creek has a history of the families of the Campbell's and Plott's who were among the early settlers. The Sutton's also had a lot of land in the early years of the community of Maggie Valley. Carpenter's Branch on Sheep Back Mountain was the home of the Carpenter family, one of the early families in Maggie Valley. The Jacob Setzer family settled in Setzer's Cove.

There was an amusement park on a knob of Buck Mountain. Ghost Town in the Sky had a chair lift and rail ride that went straight up the mountain. It had been there for about fifty years. Another place of note is the Cataloochee

The childhood home of Maggie Setzer, for whom the town of Maggie was named, 1904. *Courtesy of the* Enterprise Mountaineer.

Ranch. Tom and Judy Alexander were the first to own and develop the ranch. The permanent ranch land was bought in 1938. It covers a thousand acres on three ridges. The ranch opened in June 1939. In 1961, the ranch became year round and provided skiing in the winter. Then in 1968 the Cataloochee Ranch relocated to a larger area, where it is today. Mr. Tom died in 1972 and Miss Judy died in 1997. The Alexander family still manages the ranch, which is open all year.

Bibliography

Primary Information

Mr. Charley Way, grandson of Dr. J.H. Way. Interview by Janet Webb.

Public or Official Documents

Government and Business Services Branch, State Library of North Carolina. *North Carolina Laws.* Chapter LXI, 1810.

Office of the Registrar of Deeds, Haywood County Courthouse. *Haywood County Deed Book A.* Waynesville, NC.

———. *Haywood County Maps*. Waynesville, NC.

———. *Haywood County Quarter Session Court Minutes*. Waynesville, NC.

———. *Haywood County Will Books*. Waynesville, NC.

Newspaper

Haywood County *Enterprise Mountaineer.*

Books

Allen, W.C. *The Annals of Haywood County North Carolina*. 1935. Reprint, Spartanburg, SC: The Reprint Company, 1982.

———. *Centennial of Haywood County and Its County Seat, Waynesville, N.C.* Waynesville, NC: Courier Printing Company, 1908.

Arthur, John Preston. *Western North Carolina: A History from 1730 to 1913*. 1914. Reprint, Johnson City, TN: Overmountain Press, 1996.

Blackmun, Ora. *Western North Carolina: Its Mountains and Its People to 1880*. Boone, NC: Appalachian Consortium Press, 1977.

Frome, Michael. *Strangers in High Places: The Story of the Great Smoky Mountains*. Garden City, NY: Doubleday, 1966.

Hunter, Cyrus L. *Sketches of Western North Carolina Historical and Biographical*. 1877. Reprint, Bowie, MD: Heritage Books, Inc., 1995.

Powell, William S. *North Carolina Through Four Centuries*. Chapel Hill: University of North Carolina Press, 1989.